THE FRUGALIST

INDIE BOOKSHOP EDITION

#littleoldladywho

Publishing Data
First published 2020 Sliding Scale Books (SSLOLW01)

Plaza De Andalucía 1, Campofrío, 21668, Huelva, Spain.

ISBN 978-84-122029-0-8

Dedicated to my

*Y.H. (Young Hubby) because my riches come
from contentment and mutual support*

CONTENTS

INTRO – ABOUT THE AUTHOR

Usually, an author biog goes at the end, but I need to introduce my 'frugal credentials'. I'm not one of those middle class 'down-sizers'. In fact I've spent rather a lot of my life trying to upsize on very limited means. I've spent almost all my 40+ years of adulthood as an artist and have only worked for other people for less than five years of that working life. Only one year have I earned over 20 thousand pounds clear. For a good deal of my life, I've lived at, or under what would be considered poverty level. I've been a single parent, some of this time on benefits but most of it working for myself in creative businesses. Nevertheless, I've travelled extensively, eaten of the best and brought up three children mostly in a deprived area to be strong, intelligent, well educated and responsible adults. I've also renovated and self-built my way to a lovely, if a bit unfinished, home in Andalusia. We still have some financial issues trying to get off grid; but that's another story. Also, for much of this time, I've beaten myself up about the things I didn't do and the things I didn't give my children. Often found myself on the defensive for taking a road less travelled. But a recent life-threatening illness, followed by conversations with friends who have done things in life in an ostensibly more 'responsible' way have made me realise not only that I didn't actually do anything wrong, but more than that, that I did things almost entirely right, but that this isn't the only way.

Recently one of my oldest friends, who I'd refer to as "differently frugal" and I were chatting over a cup of tea in her lovely French house which she struggled all her life to get, by dedicating herself to a successful career as a lawyer. In a conversation about my current situation, she suddenly blurted out "I would have liked to have been an artist and travelled". Perversely, she then went on to suggest that people who did what I did were feckless. At first I was floored by, and defensive at the comment but I knew I wasn't feckless … in fact, if there were such a thing as 'feck' I probably have too much of it. When I asked her to define 'feckless' what she actually described was 'reckless'. I would have to admit I have been that, at times, sometimes resulting in much steeper mountains for myself to climb. I have been penniless and single, and depressed and anxious. Yet I have recovered from all of these situations and I have almost never had to go to work for someone else. And all improvements to my situation were almost all in my own hands, and of course, so were hers. We are not so very different, but we believed, as a result of our different environments, in our own way of getting to the same goals.

My friend, in her own words, is naturally thrifty and obsessive. I know I could best be described as naturally wild and spendthrift (when able to be so). She is now doing the things she always wanted to in life within the freedom of financial security. I had been doing all the things I wanted to all my life, but now do not have that same security. As far as completing on the mission to be financially secure she has definitely beaten me to it. I will almost certainly never reach that place. As far as completing on our mission to create and leave behind something of ourselves in this world well, I've smashed it and my friend is just starting on some of that. Even as best friends we can look sideways and wonder if each other got it more right. I'm happy now, that I got it right ... for me and that she got it right for her. But I now have some payback to do by continuing to work and she has some rewards to reap by getting to play around at last! Our frugality has been different. Hers was self imposed and mine was either absent ... or imposed. Now she has to learn to let go a bit. I have to learn to rein in a bit more.

In my village in Spain, my neighbours, especially the young families have 'got with the programme.' They are desperately working to educate their kids into finding jobs all over the world. This is so that in the end they all have the freedom to come back to where they started ... to enjoy retirement and die in their community. One has to ask oneself whether the middle bit is really that necessary. Their village lifestyle is now one more and more people aspire to and to me is the peak of contentment. Whether we have gone too far in seeking our ultimate goals in the roundabout way of propping up the current economic system is an important and moot point. Opening up this discussion is probably the reason I added the Anarchist 'A' in the title.

As I pull this book together, it seems that half of the world is waking up to the moral and political need not to over-consume. The other half are still addicted to the growth economy which is failing.

THE A OF FRUGALISM

You may say using the Anarchist logo is a bit 'culturally appropriating' the symbol meaning a lot more than my little work on changing things down a bit. I used it for two reasons. The first, to be honest, was that I thought it would look good on the cover. The second is the way I'm feeling right now while compiling this book. We are in what seem to be the last days of the great Brexit takeover of our freedom not to work every hour of every day for the benefit of "The Man". I do feel my inner Anarchist coming out a little more. Although clearly I'm actually a socialist and a voter! I've fought a good fight against Brexit and still don't know whether we've won or lost all control of democracy or our own personal battle to stay living in Spain. I don't know whether Brexit is merely a bubble blip before the business of quietly asset stripping the lot of us continues at its more usual slow pace. My gentle message of frugality making life just a bit easier may still turn into an act of out and out rebellion, who knows? All I can say is that the more society lurches into capitalism, the more I don't want to play that game. My hope is that wherever you are on the naturally/unnaturally frugal spectrum, if you want to or need to pare down your spending there will be a few ideas here for you. You can be mean, green or in between. All the changes you make you should make only because you want to. I do hope there's something in here that pays you back for the few quid you paid for the book (or less for the ebook). Or something than makes you think about your consumption.

There are lots of anarchists who are also freegans, squatters and money-less or partly moneyless livers. I'm not one of those, but I am sympathetic to their cause. They are like the high priests of frugal anarchy. Personally I don't want to practise that much religious fervour! In fairness I should lay out the political reasoning behind my assertion that you are doing a good political thing by being more frugal.

Consumerism supports an increasingly corrupt and unjust system. The way the profiteers keep you hanging on and living in that system is to keep you craving things you really don't need. They keep you in fear of losing things you really don't need while they slyly rob you of, or tax you for, things you really do! Relative poverty is a thing. As long as we try to keep up with or even exceed the 'Joneses', failing makes us unhappy, even if we already have everything we really need.

There is a problem with rejecting consumerism if you have children. They live in the same areas and go to the same schools as people who buy in to 'keeping up with the Joneses'. I have never been forgiven for not buying my own teenage son a pair of Nike Air Jordans. That was the must-have footwear for his age group back in the 80s. Anyone who didn't have the correct trainers would be quite literally bullied and derided for it. I didn't buy them because I couldn't afford them,. That explanation didn't help him a lot. It did highlight the injustice when I knew that some of his friends had these coveted items and the smart bike and the top end computer games machines as the result of crime. I think if we're going to reduce crime we have to look at equality of opportunity. I am almost sympathetic as to how this 1980s 'greed is good' unfairness can make a parent even resort to crime to provide their kids with what they relatively 'need'. I wouldn't go there, but I think you have to attempt to allow your children to fit in, if you live in that kind of community; if you simply can't then you have to be really strong and respect and understand the pressures on your kids can be immense.

So now its time to get a bit political-ranty. Personally I think the only reason to have a government is to make the world a fairer and more stable place. Currently the government of the day are failing spectacularly on both counts. I agree with paying taxes in order to achieve order and a welfare state but not in order to have wealth redistributed upwards. If we have a fair and just system we should all be delighted to be able to pay our share each according to his ability. I have no sympathy at all with people who only want to pay for what they individually get the benefit of. That's not how community works.

At the moment, not least because of all the hidden taxes, the tax burden is actually falling the hardest on the poorest in society. The notion that the poor are poor because they are in some way defective, is pure narcissism by those with an inherited wealth advantage and merely kept and increased it in a system of their own making.

It is however perfectly possible, legal and ethical to pay a much smaller level of tax and also benefit the planet by consuming less and simply refusing to engage in the FOMO (fear of missing out) culture. That's a pretty good way of being part of the resistance to neo-liberal politics and planetary damage.

Poverty is impoverishing to society and to the planet both in absolute terms and because of the way we buy into the consumerist society. But only if we all buy into it. Everyone who manages to get their happy life balance right, sticks two fingers up at the wrong side of current politics and yet does no harm.

This book is not a manifesto for green and clean and perfect living, nor is it really an anarchist handbook. There's unfortunately little I can do about the major injustice perpetrated by governments cutting benefits and removing peoples rights.

So here I am on the edge of 'frugalism', and dipping my toes into anarchy. Having been a bit short or a lot short of money all my life apart from a few short years when I was selling rather a lot of my craft products somehow, because of some frugal and some reckless behaviour I keep managing to climb out of poverty. The one 'big year' of my business' major success was not without its problems, though. I was working from dawn to midnight seven days a week and I was stretching myself way too thin and my health suffered. Was it worth it? It's difficult to count against the crash which took away all the flexibility we'd gained and plunged us back into debt. We won and we lost. It was, it seemed, always like that. Somehow however, I've lived a full and interesting and almost always happy life in the process of my own financial and emotional ups and downs.

In this book I try not to preach anything and neither do I always follow a strict path myself. I have no frugal mantras, no rules, and I don't care if you think this book is the bees knees or just find one little idea that makes life just a little easier. I'll be happy either way. I'm aware that this book may also annoy a lot of people. It will annoy people who have even less money, mental health or flexibility than I have had in my life, and it will annoy those with more. I have to be understanding of that because its part of the human condition to be judgemental and to make comparisons. My ideas for a more frugal existence are only gleaned from my own experience. These are worked out usually more out of necessity than a real desire to live in a particular way and of course some may not work for you. Some of my choices may annoy some people where they show that we have been, as my mother would have said, 'sailing a bit close to the wind'.

Another thing I need to say straight off. I am not going to attempt to tell you how to live off a pound a day or 50 pence!!! There are several Facebook groups dedicated to that subject. I'm horrified that people have to try to do that and have a great deal of empathy for their/your plight. We all have days where that's all there is though, so I hope in the recipes section there are a few ideas to help. I don't advocate living off potatoes and pasta long term but maybe there are other ideas which might help you (benefit cuts apart) to make sure there is just a little more money to spend on nutrition. If you want to help someone living on a stupidly low income like this, a jar of multi-vitamins or a dozen eggs may be a more useful gift than another bag of pasta or a pound coin. There may of course be people who disagree with me on this, but I was given both the eggs and the vitamins when I had next to nothing, and those gifts were very helpful. Even more importantly they meant the world to me because they showed that those friends were actually thinking of me, and my needs. Be kind to yourself and if you can, be understanding of each other.

WHAT STOPS US BEING FRUGAL?

There are days when we just can't stop ourselves and that's OK. The more frugal you are, the more you can get away with the odd what I call 'spendfest'. I do one every now and then. I'll either go into a supermarket with an extra handful of money and just get whatever I want, or I'll buy a bigger item that I've been thinking about for a while. Some of those bigger items are detailed later.

But there are things which will make us spend more just to be in with the in crowd. Often these are at public and social occasions where we feel forced to pay our round or stay in a particular hotel or offer to buy a meal or a present that we simply can't afford. Often we may avoid the situations altogether to avoid the fallout but we really should be able to stand our frugal ground against social pressures and enjoy community and social occasions without feeling undermined.

Judgemental attitudes and language towards frugal behaviour can be ignored or deflected. People love to judge and criticise. Generally the reason for this is that they are not entirely comfortable with their own life choices and its more comfortable for them to balance theirs with yours and find negative ways to view yours. We all get sucked into these behaviours especially when we feel defensive or belittled. Consciously or unconsciously most of us bend a little to what are considered to be 'norms' and there is language used against anyone who is seen to be eccentric in any way to try to pressure us into either behaving in a way that makes people feel more comfortable, or to make us hang our heads and slope off from the crowd. This is quite common in the subject area of how and where when and how much we choose to earn and spend our money. When you choose to be, or even are forced to be frugal you are going to be challenging other peoples world view on a pretty fundamental level. If your frugality is not personal choice your very existence challenges them to find reasons why you are less deserving of a higher income or more of the obvious trappings of wealth. Even if your frugality is so that you can make choices that they haven't made, people are often drawn to make comparisons about your choices and theirs.

It is important to remember that being judgemental is a fundamental human condition and their problem not yours. Here though, are a few of the words people choose to make themselves feel better about their spending choices by referring to yours in the negative. Just reading through them and half expecting them will help you prepare to deflect any negativity towards your choices or let them pass over you.

Negative language includes tightwad or simply tight, close fisted, skinflint, mean, cheap, parsimonious, abstemious, sparing, penny-pinching, stinting. There are a couple more which I have not included because they are racially offensive however, niggardly (noun: niggard) is an adjective meaning "stingy" or "miserly". It is derived from the Middle English word nigard, which is probably itself derived from an old Norse word hnoggr ("stingy"). It is however unlikely to be used these days because of its phonetic similarity to a racial slur.

Neutral or positive comments can also be used as negatives in a sarcastic exchange. We should cheerfully thank people for any comments along these lines and refuse to be drawn into that kind of negativity. Careful, economical, economising, thrifty, abstinent, temperate, saving, choice, chary, penny-wise, prudent and of course frugal.

Antonyms include: lavish, spendthrift, prodigal profuse, luxurious, extravagant, indulgent, self-indulgent, intemperate, short-sighted, improvident, rash, profligate, squandering, thriftless, wasteful.

You can use these to deflect any negatives. Just give them the "as opposed to" defence, smile and walk away. Admittedly that's getting into the comparison game, but hey … radical acceptance isn't for everyone!

A FRUGAL MINDSET. BE PREPARED.

There are so many reasons you may want to go frugal. There may be many reasons why you were attracted to this book. Defining those reasons may motivate you, help you to decide the level of frugality you want or need and to set achievable goals.

"When you are young, you have time and health but no money.
When you are working, you have money and health but no time.
When you are old, you have time and money but no health".
Attrib: Luisa May Alcott

What if we stopped chasing the dollar so hard and learned to appreciate time more throughout the whole of our lives?

Whatever the reason you need or want to become frugal, frugality frees you from the constraints that living an 'ordinary life' place on you. The first thing you need to free is your mind. You need to free yourself from the entirely false idea that you must live the kind of life your relatives, friends and society expects of you. It may just be that they don't have all the answers. And it may just be that they actually envy your simpler life and are unconsciously making themselves feel better by judging you to be wrong in your life path.

Maybe you just don't feel the need for so much money

I once had an assistant working for me who used to come in to work only when she needed the money. This infuriated me especially as I paid her very well per hour and had plenty of work for her. Why didn't she want to earn some of this almost endless potential pot? I thought. But why should she change her mind? She earned the money she needed for her minimal needs and appreciated her own time more than the extra income. Was she lazy or wise? I now think she was wise.

You have to be able not only to tell yourself but to really believe in the idea that this is an adventure in living the very best. You're not just living for less but positively giving back time and adventure and sustainability to your life. If you're that way inclined, you can stick two fingers up to a system that appears to force you into buying more and more 'stuff' just to feed their profit and taxation machines.

What ever your reasons, my number one piece of advice is to make sure you don't feel 'deprived'. This may be a new way of living, but it shouldn't be devoid of treats. You just need to pick your treats more carefully and rule out rubbish treats which cost a lot and have little value. Treats will appear throughout this book and are everyday things which give you joy, whether it be food travel or pastimes that you enjoy.

That Japanese idea that if something doesn't 'give you joy' you don't need it is a pretty smart one. When you get into this mindset, you not only don't need it, you'll find you don't want it either. This can also be applied to dieting which you will see later.

It may help you to define your reasons to help motivate you and to help you to decide the level of frugality you want and to set achievable goals.

You can live as you want and the problems that current society put on you are lessened the less you use the 'standard' way of living. You don't have to be a 'kook' (although some people may argue that I am one) and you can take the alternative lifestyle to whatever level you want. At the end of the day the most important two lessons you can learn are taking responsibility for your own actions and rolling with the punches!

Frugality out of necessity

Because you're living off benefits, off a very limited income or you have debts. Maybe you have an impending crisis. Perhaps you're already in crisis and don't know what else to do. You have an illness, have lost your job or want to make a redundancy payment stretch as far as possible. You may have realised that changing some of your habits might help you get through or even climb out of your current crisis.

Frugality towards or at retirement

Maybe like me you're one of the older generation, about to retire on a very small pension or looking at the possibility of no pension at all. We are supposed to feel anxious about this even though for many of us it's too late to plan. For others, those careful savings may have dissipated into some scam or scheme or loss of value through low interest rates and high cost of living rises. Or this money simply disappears into care home fees. You may find yourself overworking and saving to give an inheritance to the next generation but now realise that meanwhile they are being deprived of a family life which might be more valuable. Your family may themselves need less of your help in the future if they aren't deprived of the value of your time now.

Nevertheless, the young are now exhorted to put enormous amounts away to pay for a retirement they might never reach, and to want things now that they can't afford if they do save. They are being pulled in two directions at once and are made to feel guilty whichever choices they make. We are conditioned by the neo-liberal acquisitive generation, to feel that more money means a better life, and that just enough is not enough. Is that really true? What do we do with that money but buy things to make us feel better about the lack of time we have for ourselves and each other?

Frugality because you want to work less hard and want to get more out of life

Each hour you work for an employer or for yourself if self-employed taxes you. It taxes you mentally and physically and it taxes you as the taxation part of your income. So one benefit of living frugally is how many less hours you need to work to make a living. Another, how much further your free time could go in terms of quality of life. This might be time to spend with your kids or parents or loved ones. Quite apart from the fact that if you live very frugally indeed, your earnings level has a much lower percentage of tax. Every single item you don't buy means less tax paid. You may think that it costs more in time to grow a piece of fruit or a vegetable but some cost very little. The work is cheaper and more satisfying than a workout in the gym and your produce is infinitely more wholesome and the fresh air and exercise is more beneficial to your health than a car ride to Waitrose for a pot of low fat yogurt and a trip to the gym. You aren't losing anything. You're gaining a lot!

Frugality in order to spend quality time with the kids

Parents can no longer keep sick kids at home and have to send them to school or pay childminders to do what our parents could do naturally, just look after their own sick children when we needed it.

Grandparents are having to fill the childminding gap when often they would like to have more quality and less obligatory time as childminders. Those families with grandparents who are sick or have died or are living at some distance are disadvantaged. In the past having living grandparents was a positive advantage now its just a defence against an unfair society.

However spending more time with the kids may come at the cost of spending less money on them. Do you think that may be a problem? You may not be giving your kids the best of everything if they aren't enjoying the best of you.

Maybe you're buying a home and want to pay your mortgage off quicker. More and more people these days are dipping below a poverty line and those who aren't are noticing that they are working harder for less. One defence against this is to get your mortgage out of the way as quickly as possible in order to have more freedom further down the line.

Maybe you want to invest that money in a business and don't want to fritter it unnecessarily.

You could be preparing to be frugal because you can see difficult times ahead. You're OK at the moment but are planning ways to make your money stretch further.

Frugality to save for a big blowout

You might be using frugal means to save for a holiday or a necessity you can't afford like dental work or a car.

Frugality as a green agenda and frugality as resistance

This one is very interesting as we are now living in what definitely would be called a dystopian society. Using money is propping up the monetary system that has us in its binds. The taxation system is unfair to the poorest members of society and benefits most those with the least to lose. Engaging as little as possible with the act of buying and selling products which support that system is a small but significant act of anarchy or rebellion. Its not that we shouldn't want to pay tax into a fair system, but if the system doesn't benefit those at the bottom who need the most help up, then we have to help ourselves and our poorer neighbours up by old fashioned means, like creating our own goods and bartering and sharing.

Identify the positive

Think in terms of your levels of dedication. Do you want to be, or have to be ultra frugal? It might help to think of yourself in more positive terms: as a Frugal 'Warrior' perhaps? A master of rather than a slave to frugality. So that's the way I'll refer to that level of frugality. In the middle you're maybe a 'Frugalist' … like I am: talking a good fight but not always completely devoted to the 'cause'. And if you're a frugal beginner it might help to think of yourself as a 'Small-Changer'. To be honest I skip between all levels depending on my income and there's a bit of me that is utterly spendthrift! Whichever level you're at whether through choice or necessity frugality is going to make a change to your life. Its going to make some things slower, more deliberate, more 'mindful'.

Another thing worth asking yourself right at the outset is to what extent do you love money? It makes a difference whether you're being frugal as a way of life or as a means to use the money you have or to save for something else. Maybe, like me, you have a love hate relationship with it. Personally I want to be a frugal warrior, but I just love the feel of coins, the rustle of notes and the mad splurge on something expensive. I hate myself for it … but that's me out in the open in my undies: horrible sight believe me! Try to be honest with yourself. If you love a splurge and don't sometimes loosen the rope you are doomed to failure like a dieter who's addicted to chocolate. You may find the "Frugal Preparing" (later in this chapter) and "Frugal Xmas" (chapter 8) list sections useful. If you're going to spend big occasionally, it might as well be on a piece of equipment or something lovely but still frugal which will give you pleasure in the short term … and save you money in the long term!

Whatever your reasons to be frugal you need to understand that initially the planning can take a *lot* of time. You are going to have to decide to enjoy the process and keep giving yourself self-affirming pats on the back and a few frugal treats! If you like note-taking, maybe get yourself a diary to record your successes and or a folder to keep your contacts, suppliers, successful recipes and even receipts in.

Chores and meditation.

If you are attempting to downsize your work life and as a result earn less money you will find that everything else takes longer. There will be more 'chores' whether its mending, gardening, making or washing up.

Not all chores are horrible. Mind numbing can be meditative. I hated washing up. Now there are days when I think I hate it, but my early morning wash up is so meditative that I now find myself starting a new page or a new chapter of a piece of writing on the back of some thought that only entered my mind because I was quiet enough to let it in.

Gardening is both exercise and relaxation. We just have to let go of the idea that chores are always bad and start to cherish the quiet time and/or the exercise that chores allow us.

Do you look at a video of a guy chopping wood outside his country house and think "What a horrible chore"? Or do you long for the simple life he has. Does it look back breaking or romantic? Does he look weighed down by the cares of the world or free to think while he repeatedly brings the axe to the wood and sees his winter store of firewood grow, promising scores of warm evenings by a cosy fire? It's all a matter of perspective.

Obviously there are some chores we'd rather not have to do over and over but ask yourself whether you hate a job more than you hate the other job you'll have to do in order to earn the money to pay for it. I happily swapped 135 Euros for a robot vacuum cleaner because it gives me joy not to have to keep sweeping up after my cats and my crafts every day and suffering the asthma that can cause. However, when my dishwasher broke down I realised I didn't hate washing up half so much as I thought I did especially as I wasn't keen on the stacking either, nor the paying for the tablets and we certainly couldn't afford a new one without severe deprivation in other areas. I had got used to the idea of a dishwasher when my life was extremely busy but that in fact I had now changed my life down enough to enjoy the process of washing up since I didn't work so damned hard that I felt I needed to throw the pots in the washer and run around like a headless chicken to pay for that dubious pleasure. Yes, there were very real reasons why I'd had one before, not least of which was the unfairness of the division of household chores in my past when two ungrateful unhelpful children and ditto husband didn't take on part of the job. I have to say, things have now changed!

It helps if you see the positive side of the jobs we were always told we had to hate because maybe we just don't!

One of the investments you can make when starting on this adventure is, if you aren't already reading this on Kindle, to get a Kindle or a Kindle app on your tablet or phone if you have one . Maybe a Kindle Unlimited account for a couple of months and read books about people who walk or cycle as their lifestyle or adventure. Why do I suggest Kindle? Because its a cheaper way to read and to store a lot of books. You may just rediscover the joy of reading yourself to sleep. This is a lot easier if you aren't disturbing a loved one with your bedside lamp antics. It's a big outlay for someone on a very restricted budget but if you can, I believe you should … If nothing else, reading about other lives can take your mind out of cyclical thinking about the toughest parts of your own.

Change your mind.

Another thing you can do to help yourself get into the right mindset is strangely to throw things out (or rather give stuff away). This includes physical 'things' and also negative psychological habits.

This obviously assumes that you have more than enough for your needs to consider thinning out.

One of the problems that often holds us back is the idea that more 'stuff' makes us happier. If you're a hoarder you'll find it actually makes you less happy to be surrounded by clothes and shoes that you'll never wear and toys or devices that you will never use. Give the clothes that don't fit and the extra sleeping bags or quilts, etc. to the homeless or to other charities or recycling schemes (preferably in that order). You might find it difficult to actually hand something over to a homeless person. If so, just take it to a bin or recycling area that's close to where homeless people sleep, and leave it close to that facility. Not in the bin but on it, or beside it. You may wish to write the words "Free - please take" on the bag. This is a great exercise. One of the things which will free you from the idea that in living a frugal lifestyle makes you less worthy than your rat-race running neighbour, is to learn not to be so judgemental yourself. Everyone has their own story. We don't know what circumstances have brought your homeless neighbour to the streets. If you're thinking "probably drink or drugs" then ask yourself what childhood horrors or accident of fate may make someone choose the beginning of that slope. Be grateful that you didn't suffer those horrors or were lucky to have the strength to overcome them. If you are naturally judgemental, forgive yourself because it isn't your fault either … but it *is* your responsibility.

So what don't you need? Start with clothes you never wear. *But* if the reason you've kept them is that you love them, but sadly they don't fit any more you might need to consign them to a drawer. If you're following my diet tips or even if you realise that eating better food makes you naturally lose weight, you may well find that after a while you can visit your own drawer or storage box to go clothes 'shopping' again. I did!

YOUR TIME AS VALUE.

First of all lets value *your* time in monetary terms. Even if money is not a notion that you have any respect for, simply having numbers to play with can help you to balance your work and personal lives. How do you do that? It's difficult because if you've been a stay-at-home parent, unemployed or an artist or lived in a low income family you may have learned that your time has little value, but that's not true because our time is worth exactly as much as the next person even the very very rich. Every hour of your life has an immense and incalculable value, however we often treat it as valueless. The whole notion of self-esteem is not one that needs covering here, lets just take this as a universal truth that everyone's time is valuable. In order to understand how we can improve our lives, we have to give our hours a notional value which we can change at any time preferably upwards. Or once we truly understand the value of time we can abandon the idea of monetary value altogether.

If you are already employed, you can value your time as either the gross or net value of your working hours, just as a starting point. If you are unemployed or an artist don't think that your time has a lesser value. You can value it at the level at which you would have a comfortable life if you worked for, say, a 35 hour working week.

Just for the sake of argument, I'm going to value time at 25+ pounds / euros / dollars an hour. I'm not going to go into exchange rates as this is just a notional value. If you feel that's too much you can adjust it down, but don't start too low. If I can 'get more' for a working hour then

I'm quids in. If I don't get paid for it then I have gained an hour that's worth 25 'units'. If I'm doing something for someone else for nothing then I'm giving them a gift of my time at that value. If I want to count it. But I don't need to because I'm already comfortable with both the notions that time is valuable and that a gift is a gift and comes with no strings attached. It also helps me value other peoples time and helps me to know whether I'm being ripped off or not. It helps me decide whether I want to have a go at something myself or I want to value someone else's training, ability and speed at the job a bit more highly. If it would take me longer and I would probably be crap at it then I'm happier to leave it to the experts and pay them for it. Whether that's fixing teeth, cars, human bodies, or designing houses etc. We also have to remember that many people have invested unpaid time into honing skills that we just don't have. But equally as an artist and author I'm now able to value the time I've spent building up my skills. Researching, evaluating, failing and succeeding. No longer do I need let people speak of my work as if I were just playing or avoiding real work. My time is my time to spend in the present or invest in the future as I please.

No longer will I ever feel guilty at giving something home made with love rather than something that 'cost money'. Nor will I react defensively to a comment that my handmade gift of miniature flowers, were cheaper than the real thing; because I know they weren't.

There is, however, a question of rest, including sleep. You might be asking yourself whether you can allow yourself an hour of siesta given that your hours are worth 25+ units. Let's deal with this simply by saying that rest and sleep equals health. You simply can't place a value on health because without it nothing else works. So we should divide off, say 10-12 hours of each day for sleep and other rest and make that sacrosanct and literally invaluable.

You can give a negative value to a chore by deducting the time taken to do it. That may be balanced by giving a positive value to the pleasure or exercise gained by doing it. My washing up chore mentioned earlier, for example. I now run backwards and forwards to note down ideas while I'm washing up. This is also good for my exercise! You can also add back the value of the benefit you may be giving back to other peoples improvement in health or welfare. After all, you're not taking so much from the planet.

All these thought processes help you not to undervalue yourself and also, just as importantly, not to overvalue someone who ostensibly has a more important job.

There is the other question that all this revaluing throws up which is how to value your work as an artist or writer, etc. Or how to ask for a raise if you're underpaid. I'll deal with this separately in the chapter on life planning.

FIND FRUGAL FRIENDS!

British reserve can be a damaging thing when it comes to poverty. Neighbours can make each other's lives easier and cheaper. I've learned that a little neighbourly support goes a long way from when my Spanish neighbours rallied round when I was sick. Very moving for me. Very normal for them. Quite apart from simply cultivating friendships and offering to help out in a crisis, there are other things you can do to help each other out. At the same time make life easier for yourselves. Win-win! And you can start small just by offering to share a bulk buy.

A neighbourhood bulk buying club is a group of neighbours that join together to purchase goods in bulk to get lower prices. It has other unseen benefits. Quite a lot of the money you save is from the iniquitous VAT (IVA in Spain). If you buy in smaller quantities, you are paying a higher price per kilo or litre etc. and of course a lot more tax too. This is because in cutting and packing them into smaller quantities they are 'upsold' or to put it another way, so called 'value' is added. Of course there is no extra value here there is only extra cost, extra packaging, extra transport and selling costs. So by buying in bulk, a lot of your savings are on VAT. And on the planet. So buying in bulk may please your inner angry anarchist as well as your purse.

Quite a few of the frugal alternatives, especially the household and medicinal items are very cheap indeed. Unfortunately, partly because they are so cheap per kilo they have to be bought in very large quantities to get the best price. For example my husband bought me my first kilo of Epsom salts as part of a birthday bath product making DIY kit. Incidentally, this was a great choice of birthday presents because it took a little time to research and some love to put together. It helped me with my frugal process and replaced my love of Lush products. I went on to make some presents for people I love with it too but of course that meant I rapidly ran out of Epsom salts. We then found buying 3 x 6 kilos came out MUCH cheaper per kilo but I happened to have just received a PPI refund so I could invest in a few things. Most people on most days can't do that, but you can share with friends.

Bulk buy foods

When I was young, my dad and his friends organised a bulk buying scheme where they bought crates of fruit from the fruit traders. One week they would share a crate of oranges, another week a crate of apples. Someone needs to cultivate a business relationship with the suppliers of course but all neighbourhood schemes are a slightly heavier burden on the organiser. Share these duties out with one organising veg (maybe direct from the farmer), one of you handling fruit from the importer, one household products etc. This community spirit can also help when bulk buying for events.

For fruit and veg you can look out for independent farmers in your area who will sell in bulk to your group.

Look at Crowdfarming.

Think about getting a group Costco card.

Set up your own semi-official group

assets.publishing.service.gov.uk/government/uploads/system/uploads/attachment_data/file/318811/12-593-guide-for-community-buying-groups.pdf

Buy heating oil together. Put 'community oil buying scheme' then your county or region into your browser if you have computer access.

LETS (Local Exchange Trading Schemes) are where friends in a neighbourhood get together and decide on the value of a skill and share one 'token value' for another. You could also call it a Skill Share Scheme. The easiest way of sharing these skills is to swap an hour for an hour. Of course you also need to factor in preparation time and perhaps even tool use or materials that you happen to have and your neighbour needs. You can get your neighbour to buy in their own materials. You don't have to love each other to bits to get into one of these schemes. But you do need something you're prepared to do upfront for 'free' or rather for a token of value that you can 'spend' with others in the group. Direct swaps are simpler and easier to understand but not always possible.

Think about the things you can do. It doesn't always have to be something obvious like electrician gardener or dressmaker it can also be baking or babysitting or sandwich making.

Think about tool sharing. We have two sections of scaffolding but to do most jobs we need three so we're prepared to lend and borrow the extra parts.

If your group gets even more co-operative who knows what tools and electrical items you might share? And what skills are connected with those tools. Wouldn't it be amazing if you could make a bread loaf for your neighbour in return for a wash load being done for you for example?

I have students who learn English from me whose parents sell firewood. A straight swap of firewood for classes. How nice and how co-operative. Another neighbour does painting work for classes.

Look up: The Slow movement

en.wikipedia.org/wiki/Slow_movement_(culture)

This group collects and distributes left over useable foods:

fareshare.org.uk

FRUGAL PREPARING

To some people frugal preparers are an oddity like survivalists but there are very good reasons to prepare to smooth out the financial cycles. You may feel that people may think of you as a bit 'daft' but you won't feel as daft when there's a strike, a redundancy, an illness, lean months for the self-employed or some other financial shock. All of these seem even more likely these days given the way the welfare state is going in the UK. And if anyone you know is in crisis you will find your emergency store makes it easier to give what is needed.

Food items

When you have extra money stock up on the following foods, and keep them in a reasonably cool dry place.

Tinned tomatoes, tinned condensed or evaporated milk, tinned coconut milk, tinned sardines or pilchards or tuna (if liked). Tins or jars of veggies you might put in a curry such as bamboo shoots, baby corn etc. Jars of olives red and green if liked. Tinned meat such as corned beef, tinned ham, hot dog sausage. Jars of jam (preferably home made), tinned fruit, molasses, dried fruit and salted peanuts. Watch dates on some of these. Use and replace when they come close to dates.

Jars of pickle Branston pickle, dill pickles, etc. (or home made pickles).

Non-food

Wash powder, washing up liquid.

'Big ticket' items

Electrical items:- I have put these on the Xmas present list section towards the back of the book. Always keep your eyes on the second hand shops and auction sites because you might be able to get them at the right price when you have enough to buy them. *A heating food processor, a vacuum sealer* and believe it or not *a robot vacuum cleaner.* A *toaster* is also useful if you don't have one because many delicious nutritious meals can be made as toast toppings. I also find a *slow cooker* brilliant for cooking Iberian pig tongues to make pressed tongue at around 2 euros a kilo.

DIY

A hand drill,

A big tin of paint for your walls and gloss paint for your woodwork, and paint brushes. These are because when you have no work you have time to refresh the house. It will be something to take your mind off it and the best time to do it!

And if you don't already have them, a *Japanese style saw and a set of screwdrivers. A box each of good quality short and medium length screws, and some wall plugs.*

Clothes

Merino wool socks, T shirts and jumpers or cardigans. These are expensive but so worth having you should keep your eyes open for second hand or on offer.

A few extra blankets and a quilt or two. An extra pair of winter shoes or boots in each adult in the family's size. An extra waterproof coat each.

Covid Virus Update

I have realised that I should have included surgical level alcohol in the emergency cupboard as well as face masks and gloves. I had all of the above anyway because of my own health needs and because of my craft work. I also happened to have a full face cover which I got with my chainsaw. It hadn't occurred to me how few people have these items on hand!

SHOPPING

Even the word shopping can bring tears to your eyes if you are really struggling. I apologise in advance for any idea that we can all afford to 'stock up' because frankly its insulting to compare people's shopping choices when you have a secure and predictable income with those when your income is irregular. High income frugality and low income frugality are two completely different things. Low income frugality is much more difficult and its really about surviving from day to day. There is little chance to make 'intelligent choices' and 'buy in bulk' when your back is against the wall. Similarly, the question of simply 'shopping online' and putting your credit card into a website can, for some, just be a different world. These shopping and stocking your store sections have ideas for everyone. Some of the bulk buys you would have to find friends to do with you if you are on an extremely tight income. Other items you might be able to buy one at a time.

You can buy direct from the producer locally, this can be one of the most expensive forms although but its also likely to be healthier. I did struggle with whether I should have put the explanation of the nutritional value of fresh food before the shopping section. It seems that this fits better in chapter 3, so you might want to skip to the first part of chapter 3 before making buying choices if you can currently give any thought to nutrition. It is worth speaking to local farmers or local farmers market type shops and asking if they have an end of the day discount, especially if you have a freezer. They might even be prepared to call you and tell you what they have a glut of. Otherwise supermarket offers especially 'ugly veg' boxes should be top of your shopping list.

Shopping online

Shopping online or in person is something I've recently been re-evaluating for several reasons. The first is that my mother in law is now elderly and infirm. We live a long way away from her and have recently set up a Tesco account delivered not only to her door but directly into her kitchen. But even if we were still doing our own weekly or monthly shop in England we'd have to think about the time taken, the petrol costs and the likelihood of being tempted by the products on the shelves 'merchandised' to look appealing to the casual shopper. Although we're bombarded with images of appealing items on our social media, we're already subject to that every day and it is something we have to deal with separately anyway. When shopping for my mother in law it's easy. We simply buy what she asks for and nothing else. After all it's her money and we aren't tempted in the same way. Applying that same idea to our own shopping list might be easier for us now especially as we're already budget conscious from our years of frugal living. I do remember many times when we lived in England and we used to go to Sainsbury's without so much as a shopping list and came home with whole trolleys full of stuff we hadn't planned to buy and didn't need. Years later when we moved out some of that 'stuff' was emptied out of cupboards and straight into the bin and I blanch thinking about how much we threw away during those non-frugal years. Not having a firm shopping list is extremely costly. I found that out even when I was on a 3-month food bank system here in Spain where we were permitted around 100 euros worth of goods for 20 euros once a month for 3 months, we had to choose the products ourselves and pay for them at the reduced prices. I was having chemo at the time and was very sick. If I were to make the list again, I would choose quite different items. Since I didn't know precisely what was available I simply said "Buy stuff like … " and gave my husband and best friend a rudimentary and non-specific list of the kinds of things that might keep and be useful over the summer months when we knew we would have almost zero income that year. Even though we were dreadfully badly off it was difficult to shop carefully with so badly written a list and they came home with some products which were unusable or which didn't get used. This just illustrates the fact that if you have an idea what you need and then can compare it with what's available, you can make better decisions. Of course the first time you shop online is always going to be the one that costs you the most time, both in setting up and decision making.

Should I shop online?

You do need to ask yourself whether the trip to the shop gives you pleasure and exercise or not, and whether the extra time, money and petrol costs spent on shopping 'live' is worth the extra investment. The delivery charges can be factored in of course but on a large shop these are very small if you factor in the time (and money) saved after the first shop. Of course online shopping may give you no pleasure at all, so that does have to be balanced. Also online shopping you can't visit the 'bargain bins' which do deliver around 30% savings and, for me at least, lots of pleasure!

In the end the only way you can really know if it works for you is to try it with frugality as one of your major evaluating factors. Where we live its currently not available and I would miss the beautiful drive to our nearest town anyway. Plus I have a choice of more than one supermarket side by side. So for us it's a no ... for now at least. Though for my mother in law it's a virtual and perhaps even a real lifesaver.

Paying in Pounds or Euros (or Dollars, etc.) when shopping online, or abroad. Which is cheaper?

Well, sometimes it depends on the exchange rate. But for Europe wide companies it depends on the exchange rate on the day the price was 'locked in' on a catalogue. For example, a short time ago I was shopping for hinges for an IKEA unit and a pack of 4 hinges was £7.99. Bought in Spain the same pack cost 5,99 Euros. Clearly the Euro price was significantly cheaper! That's OK. Although postage costs can eat up any saving on heavy items, it can be well worth purchasing items while on holiday or working with a friend in Europe, and 'swapping the shopping'. Saving up items until it's worth sending a parcel.

Because my husband is a vegetarian with a particular liking for curry, we buy spices and certain types of lentils in the UK; along with custard powder, gravy powder and tea of course. Curry powders are rare and expensive here so we stock up whenever we're in the UK.

In the other direction, it's much cheaper to buy certain commonly prescribed drugs direct from the Pharmacy here. I take Ventolin to the UK for family members with asthma so they don't have the exorbitant prescription costs. It may be that this is technically on the edge of legal. It certainly isn't immoral!

About twice a year we have a parcel sent from the UK with our UK 'shopping'. 20 Kilos costs not much more than £1 per kilo through some of the parcel services that re-sell the major couriers services. You just need to ask yourself if you are saving yourself £1 a kilo on your goods. If you are, you're a winner!

STOCKING THE FRUGAL STORE CUPBOARD

These are our pantry basics which we would rather not be without.

Its quite sensible to make up your own regular list to pick what you have run out of when making up a shopping list. Our favourite shopping rule is never shop on an empty stomach! Always eat something before going shopping it's difficult not to over buy if you are hungry.

Dry and long life ingredients

These are the ingredients in our store cupboard which get the most regular use.

Store these in Kilner jars if possible to keep out moths and weevils. Some dry ingredients come with critters already in and a really good idea is to freeze for 48 hours before putting in your store cupboard but do not allow to get damp.

Tea and coffee (of course!) I have decaffeinated for both and have one coffee and 3 or 4 cups of tea a day. My husband has just one coffee and lots of water. Side note on drinks. Fruit juice is not healthy no matter what you may have learned. It is a fructose filled treat only. Eat your fruit whole.

Spelt Flour (more expensive than cheap flour but nutritious) replace with ordinary flour if you must.

If you can afford it, try some rye flour, and barley flour in your bread or cakes too.

Gluten Yes Gluten. Unless you're Coeliac!

Rolled oats (or porridge oats)

Basic muesli

Spelt grains and or rolled spelt if you can afford it

Tapioca and semolina

Rice. We like basmati and Thai sticky rice the best

Dry Pasta - Tagliatelle & Spaghetti

Chick peas

Dal (split lentils) cheaper in big packs in Asian stores

Chapati flour - cheaper in big packs in Asian stores

Cornflour

Custard powder (yes I know the main ingredient of custard powder is cornflour but its a cheap mix for a reliable custard and real vanilla is expensive)

Gravy powder

Oils

Olive oil expensive but nutritional and medicinal. We use a lot so we have the light and the extra virgin ones. My spanish friend who is a bit like a Spanish 'mum' just gave me 5 litres for Xmas. What a wonderful gift!

Plain veg oil

Tins

Tinned chopped tomatoes

Tinned coconut milk. Good quality not the light version

Tinned sardines in oil

Tinned pineapple

Check the dates on your store cupboard basics regularly.

We sometimes have extras in but they are already mentioned in the frugal preparing section.

These are the most important flavour basics in our store cupboard

My husband is vegetarian and so flavour is very important to us because to please a non vegetarian he needs to make our food really tasty. And he does!

Even though initially these items would add up to an expensive shop you can get them a few at a time and in any case they are just basic flavourings to aim for which will make your cheaper ingredients jump out and create really delicious as well as nutritious food on the cheap. In many cases spices have important nutritional benefits too so you don't need to eat bland food just because you are on a tight budget. But you may need to buy them one by one or two by two as finances allow if you're already on a very low income. If you're a frugal preparer you can buy them all at once. Some of the herbs are home grown in our case and don't forget you can swap and give herbs to your frugal friends.

General herbs and spices

Ginger, cayenne, coriander seed, turmeric and cumin seed.

Also:

Dried mushrooms – powdered. You can make this yourself or you can buy large bags of dried mushrooms in Asian shops. Find and grind your favourites. The best and most usable are Porcini (boletus) but these can be the most expensive, however the depth of flavour is intense. Or you can also make your own mushroom ketchup.

Chillis - home grown or chilli powder cheapest from Indian and continental stores.

Black pepper - best whole with a refillable grinder and much cheaper in bulk from an Asian store. (Useful combined with turmeric as anti inflammatory medicine see later)

Coriander seed - dried or powder - Note: home grown and then fresh frozen while still green, they are fantastic little bullets of flavour which my family absolutely adore!

Coriander leaf - grow or buy and freeze or sometimes available as dried leaf. If you can find it buy it because its hard to find dried. Coriander isn't universally liked so do feel free to leave this off your list if you don't like it!

Cumin seed or powder

Garlic - fresh or dried. Growing your own is fun. It takes 2 full years to grow a single clove of garlic into a big bulb of cloves. But meanwhile the greens and immature bulbs are lovely. Its so cheap in big bags here there's no excuse to grow it, except for the greens if your bag starts to sprout.

Dried fried onions.

Salt. Avoid coastal sea salt as these days it can be contaminated. Himalayan salt is more expensive but much better.

Oregano, basil, thyme, mint and rosemary. Grow at home if you can, fresh or dried. Share these around and save all your friends and family some money. Keep a jar of each for yourself.

soy sauce - dark

Vinegars - balsamic, sherry (Jerez), apple cider and rice vinegar.

Branston pickle or homemade pickle, mayonnaise.

Indian curry spices - garam masala

Asian spices - 5 spice

Thai green and red curry paste in tubs (keep in the freezer and just use a spoonful when needed.)

Fresh food shopping list

Milk or non dairy milks.

Butter and cheese (freeze when on offer)

Mozarella (freeze when on offer)

Parmesan (freeze) Stronger varieties are expensive but go further as a flavouring ingredient.

Don't buy processed cheese.

Eggs as many as you want, they keep quite well and are very nutritious and filling. Do not replenish until you are out or down to two or three eggs.

Veg - cauli, broccoli, potatoes, onions etc.

or economy veg box if available.

Fruit - bananas - we eat one banana each a day.

Citrus fruit and/or apples (calculate exactly how many you are likely to eat and don't over buy unless in season and very cheap).

Fish & meat but don't over buy.

Frozen foods

Frozen peas are the one vegetable that we would rather have frozen than fresh. We use very few but they are nicer frozen and make a lovely sweet addition to rice and soups etc.

FRUGAL CLEANING CUPBOARD LIST

Household vinegar

Bicarbonate of soda (also in medicine and hygiene list)

Castille soap (also in medicine and hygiene list)

Washing up liquid. I must admit I do buy the best-known brand.

Laundry detergent concentrated. Cheap Marsella soap version from Lidl in Spain. I do buy the liquid one. I'm allergic to many soap powders.

Active oxygen cleaner - chemical formula name Sodium Perchlorate.

Epsom salt crystals (also in medicine and hygiene list)

Kaolin powder (also in medicine and hygiene list)

Essential oils (also in medicine and hygiene list)

When you can afford to, get them in. Buy in larger containers and all of these are cheaper than you imagine. Or join with a relative or a neighbour on buying big quantities. Even though none of these items are expensive, it's still nice to save even more. Not just that but it saves on hidden eco - costs like transportation.

Basic Shopping list - Medicine chest, personal hygiene and beauty products.

For more usage information on all of these see the frugal medicine chapter 7. Some of these items are already on your food and/or household shopping lists.

Epsom salts - bathing and stomach problems (plus cleaning, fabric conditioning and gardening uses)

Shea butter - skin creams for dry and itchy skin, conditioners, etc.

Coconut oil - skin treatment and beauty creams hair oil (and cooking)

Beeswax - skin creams (and food wraps and furniture wax)

Glycerin - skin treatments (and food prep)

Bicarbonate of soda - bathing, antacid, antifungal (also cleaning and store cupboard-baking)

Aromatherapy oils - lavender oil and tea tree oil, disinfectant, calming plus many more uses

Non-nanozincoxideforbabycreamsunscreenantifungalandantiperspirant creams and powder

Cider vinegar - (already in your food cupboard) for bathing, anti mite anti head-louse, hair conditioner

Vicks Vaporub - it is possible to make something similar but for the quantity you use its simply not worth it

Aspirin - blood thinning

Paracetamol - pain control

The last four are cheapest in your supermarket. The rest can often be bought much cheaper online and some in bulk.

A few more health items which may already be in your food shopping basket or in your spice cupboard or food store. You certainly don't need to have all these in your house but they will all come up in various home made remedies.

Oatmeal or oat bran

Coconut oil

Olive oil

Honey

Lemons

Bicarbonate of soda
Herbs & spices
Cloves
Turmeric
Black pepper
Cinnamon
Cayenne pepper
Dill or fennel seed
Garlic
Sage
Peppermint essence or peppermint sweets
Ginger
Vinegar

EVERY DAY LUXURIES

There are a few everyday luxuries which I buy whenever there is at least 30% off the original price.

Butter. Whenever I can, I stock up on butter and freeze. Butter reacts well to freezing but don't try it with butter substitutes.

Parmesan cheese. Another expensive item, normally. We *have* found it in the reduced bin and of course scooped up armfuls. It also freezes well as does all cheese even Mozarella

Olive oil is almost never on a very cheap offer, but I find it vital in more ways than one. Whenever you see olive oil at the right price go for it. It can be cheaper bought in large quantities so if you have a sudden unexpected income spend some of it on olive oil. We found 3 litre bottles sold with a free ovenproof Pyrex dish. Your health and the deliciousness of your food will never regret it. Naturally, extra virgin is the best but for some people its a bit strong in flavour so you can go for a cheaper one if you need to.

We used to buy in in great big gallon containers (5 litres) at around 20 euros from a co-operative. There is a Spanish cooperative online called Olibeas. I can recommend their olive oil highly. But watch out.

Its actually no more expensive to buy it a litre at a time in many places. It can be delivered free but you have to buy a lot! Really a big family's worth or a streets worth.

After Xmas is when you can get hold of freezable fresh luxuries. I go for cheeses. Vintage cheddar and Stilton are favourites. Pork pies, speciality sausages and Xmassy presentations like 'pigs in blankets'. It's also when items like smoked salmon can be available at half the price. I buy what I can afford and separate it into one person portions. Its still not ultra frugal but it's a real treat to serve up with Philadelphia cheese on any old bread or toast, or as part of a salad.

FOOD STORAGE

Here are some ideas for making your food last longer and taste better. I learned some of them from a debt charity and took what worked for me and rejected those that didn't as you can see!

Keep your fridge clean they say. Not too difficult when its nearly empty! In the unlikely event of you actually having a smelly fridge from uneaten food, the best way to clean it is with a natural cleaning solution, try a solution of one part vinegar or lemon juice if you have home grown lemons to three parts water. Then place an opened box of bicarbonate of soda or half a lemon in it. Payplan (the debt charity) recommend using freshly ground coffee. Hmmm. That's a strange one for a frugal tip. If you drink fresh coffee (I do) keep your used coffee grounds anyway. Some of those can go in the fridge for a day or three if they're reasonably dry. However, if you eat most of your food and don't over buy fresh food, it's really unusual to have a smelly fridge! All saved leftovers can go into a glass container with a plastic lid. I'm a great fan of these in all sizes. Lidl often sells them in England and in Spain and I can get very small ones in El Jamon here. Wherever you can find them they're a great investment and a very green alternative to plastic bags or Tupperware type boxes. They can usually go almost straight from fridge to oven and vice versa. Less washing up too!

Tomatoes and courgettes are better stored at room temperature They tend to rot in the fridge. However in really hot temperatures you might need to put them in there.

Hard cheese can be kept in oil or just rubbed with oil or butter to stop it drying out. If you have kept your cheese in oil, don't waste the oil. Use it in pasta dishes.

Most frugal livers would take shop bought fresh herbs off their list.

Apparently *bananas* last longer when hung from a hook, although we get through a banana each a day so I've never tried this one. Other fruits should keep for a week or so if you don't over-buy. If you shop once a week, you should be looking at an empty fruit bowl the day before your shop anyway. If you've bought too many on offer for example, pop them in the salad drawer of your fridge and don't be tempted next time they are cheap unless you have a really good reason to buy more.

Lettuce? Don't buy iceberg or open headed lettuce, go instead for those tiny fat lettuce hearts or Romaine lettuce. Also, the little fat ones (called cogollos in Spain) are really nice halved and fried in butter. By the way butter is on my essentials list! These types of lettuce will last much longer than ordinary lettuce. But really, as my vegetarian husband says, lettuce isn't food. If you're on a tight budget, you get more nutrition for your money with broccoli. However, as a medicine lettuce can be very useful. It is a mild soporific (sleep promoter) so is useful for anxious people. Buy it from the half-price shelves and it makes a great addition to chicken soup for someone who's feeling what I call a bit 'weedy'! Its also quite high in vitamin A in case you are specifically short of that vitamin but eating half a lettuce is quite difficult. If you're a lettuce fan … go for it. But its not a cheap fix of vitamin A. You're probably better off with some Swiss chard or any number of other leafy vegetables.

Some veg like celery, broccoli and lettuce will last longer if you wrap them in a beeswax wrap if you have one.

Some people recommend aluminium foil but personally I avoid aluminium wherever possible. We have some, but our roll is maybe 2 years old.

Keep *ginger* in the freezer I buy it when its cheap and chop into lumps. You can grate it straight from the freezer.

If you like Thai curry once you've opened a pot (the bag inside the pot) keep the whole thing in the freezer and just squeeze a spoonful out when you need it. It stays soft.

Mushrooms should be kept unwashed in a paper bag. If they are unused by the time they start drying and wrinkle just speed up the drying by leaving them somewhere warm and dry. Chop any muddy ends and wipe off any soil/grit with a soft brush or paper towel first.

Eggs can be used for quite a long time after they are bought and a short while after their expiry date. If you are unsure, pop them in a bowl of water. If they lie on the bottom they're fresh, if they stand on their end in the bottom they're OK but use them up now. If they rise to the surface throw them away. If you have a glut, eggs *can* be frozen! (I have had to do this regularly when neighbours have been overly generous!) It can be best to separate the white and the yolk. Home made egg yolk custards are just lovely. You can use one egg yolk in an ordinary custard and not notice the difference except it will be a more nutritious sweet! You can also make egg white based slice-able loaf. That's all many vegetarian slices are!

EATING WELL IS FRUGAL

I'm going to say this straight away. It's understandable that busy or overstretched families will choose quantity over quality but cutting out a balanced diet which is high in fresh vegetables and fruit (note I put fruit second) is not clever nor frugal. Losing your good health will lead to greater financial problems down the line. I'm also going to say very clearly, cheap bulky high calorie, low nutrition food may 'fill you up' but it will not satisfy you. It will make you crave more as your body tries to make up for the lack of nutrition, you will gain weight and lose health. There is no more important item on my frugal advice than this. Its much much better to learn to eat less of more nutritious food. If you want to get a feeling of satisfaction, eat an egg. Seriously! (unless you are vegan).

Of course, not everyone has a garden and not everyone has a fridge nor even a cooker but if you can cook, you should, and if you can get fresh vegetables and fruit from the market or from a supermarket offer, you should.

I don't often cook now because my husband is a vegetarian and so he's the house chef and I only cook when I'm craving meat. When I was a younger single parent either working, self-employed or sometimes on benefits, the one thing I always did in those days was cook good food. And when single with my two boys I didn't allow picky behaviour. Obviously some children really dislike some things but my (old lady) answer to the problem of kids not liking things was always the same and my advice still is. That's fine … but no replacements. That is to say, they waited until the next meal. Biologically this is a very sensible approach. It served both me, and them very well and they not only love food but they love all food and aren't picky adults. It is difficult to set those rules if you haven't had them so far but 'short term pain, long-term gain' of that I have zero doubt. You can't always be a popular parent!

The food I made was cheap but nutritious and obviously I leaned more towards the vegetables that they would eat and in forms they would eat them. I also got very good at batch cooking and freezing.

We ate a lot of fishcakes made from cod cheeks which were cheap at the time. I made chicken soup from carcasses, cottage pie and fish pie. I was rather good at curries using cheaper cuts of meat and lots of lentils and I made my own fresh chapatis. Chapatis are a relatively cheap staple if you buy the flour in big bags from the Asian stores. We also ate a lot of fish fingers and burgers. I probably gave them more animal protein than they needed. Their food was almost always served with vegetables though, and we did like a pudding (not necessarily my best choice that, though!). But once again, no meal … no pud. For a treat we had home-made pizzas when cheese was in the cheap bin.

My kids have grown and gone. The boys were rarely sick and grew tall and strong. Maybe they were a little taller than they would have been. I blame that on the chicken which probably had too many antibiotics and hormones in.

My second husband and I both fell into bad habits. My interest in whether my food was healthy did slip for a while. I gained lots of weight and ate far too many fried snacks. I thought I was too busy and too poor to be disciplined about food. I did exactly what I say you shouldn't do. My habits most definitely changed again after my cancer, an illness I feel sure my very bad habits had contributed to. We are both a bit greedy and both were overweight until my illness and a chronic condition for my husband forced us to rethink our diet. Now we eat better and for less … And both of our health conditions are dramatically improved. Win-win-win!

This last couple of years we've concentrated more on home growing as a health, as well as a frugal, choice. Our garden is tidier, more productive and of course we get the exercise from it. We eat well every day now and food once again gives me real pleasure but no surplus weight.

If you don't have a garden, do check out your local market once a week or your supermarket box schemes which are becoming more and more available.

You might go through a period of feeling a bit hungry when you first give up cheap food. You will certainly lose a bit of weight initially but you will feel better and your eyes will sparkle because you will have all the essential nutrients. Those cravings for excess foods will go away when your body realises its not being starved. You might also need a multivitamin or some vitamin B (see mental health section) if your food is of the mass produced variety or is not so fresh.

Small changers: make sure you only eat healthy whole food don't buy fast food or ready meals. They are never good value and rarely high in nutrition. They are what's called 'up-sold'. Cheaper ingredients are put together and you pay double or more for the dubious privilege of the slightly shorter prep time.

Frugalists: learn some healthy frugal favourites and cycle between them. If you have a garden, get going as soon as possible. Cheaper supermarket food is not likely to be better nutritionally but look for offer boxes of veg etc.

Frugal Warriors: loads of time but no money for ingredients? Get the store cupboard basics in when you can and learn a few foraging tricks. If you don't have a cooker or even a microwave, there are things you can cook just using a kettle (see below). If you have the chance and don't have your own place to grow veggies join a gardening group.

See **www.incredible-edible-todmorden.co.uk**

Best big buy for the frugal foodie

I really do recommend a cheaper version of the robot chef type machine although I know this may be an impossibility for some as even the cheap version costs 150 pounds (though I've seen one today at 39.99 on Groupon). So they are clearly coming down in price into the level where they are affordable by most. We got ours just last year because we had a mountain of veggies coming in from the garden and I'd tried one of the expensive versions at my friends house. If you do get the chance, it can replace a mixer, smoothie maker, blender, fryer etc. and can turn a bag of veggies from a supermarket cheap bin, end of day market bargain or foraged veggies into a really nice ultra fresh hot soup without the problem of stopping and blending and splashing and scalding yourself. They seem to retain the flavour and nutrients much better than boiling in a pan. They also usually have a steaming function which is great for fish and even different paddles for bread making and beating. It's the simplest and best upgrade in cooking I've seen in decades. We've only used it for mixing pesto, for soups, curries, risotto and chopped lightly fried veggies so far but that's all we've needed it for. But if you can only afford one piece of cooking equipment I've no doubt you could cook pasta, hard boil eggs and all sorts of things in it. After all I already hard boil eggs and cook pasta in my travel kettle (wash out very well after!). So why not!

Some of my typical basic meal plans.

These are vegetarian but I do have meat and fish on occasions.

Most of these meal plans cost less than two pounds fifty per person per day including bought vegetables at a reasonable price, but not including cooking costs.

Disclaimer: These are just some of my meals using things from my garden or cheaply available locally. They are just to enable you to think about how you can lower your costs, compare and to give you a few ideas. Why not try this on your favourite foods or on some of my garden grown recipes to see if you can do them with bought veggies? Make your own recipe/cost folder and give your own favourite meals star marks.

We do tend to have around three favourites per season and change only when we get bored or find a new source or type of fresh food. I have nominally divided these into four seasons but of course they swap and change. Some are in season because that's when they would be cheaper.

Spring

Tea and coffee throughout the day

Breakfast

Lidl Crownfield basic fruit and nut muesli. In season I add fresh or frozen rasps or strawberries from the garden + half a banana, ¼ tin coconut milk

At the time of editing Crownfield basic muesli is not on the shelves. I'm currently eating porridge oats with added almonds and sultanas

Lunch

Green gazpacho.

Cucumber, 1 Italian pepper one garlic clove, one avocado, one pot natural yogurt, vinegar and olive oil, mint from the garden. Plus I slice of bread (from the freezer) and butter.

A drink of lemon juice from free lemons with honey. Lemons can be expensive out of season.

Evening

Pasta, home-made pesto (basil, olive oil) parmesan and mushrooms

A piece (or 3) of 85% chocolate

Summer

Teas and coffee throughout the day

Breakfast

Lidl Crownfield basic fruit and nut Muesli. Half a banana. In season I add raspberries, a slosh of coconut milk.

Lunch

Tagliatelle with pesto and chopped tomato

Big bunch of grapes from the garden

Evening

Black or green olive tapenade. And home-made bread

Chocolate

Autumn

Teas and coffee throughout the day

Breakfast

Lidl Crownfield basic fruit and nut Muesli, in season I add raspberries, half a banana, a slosh of coconut milk.

Lunch

Home-made soup and home-made bread

Evening

Baked aubergines with cheap cheese and parmesan + romesco sauce

This is one of the more expensive of our meals. Aubergines can be pretty expensive but you can bake any vegetable that's in season and serve with this sauce

Chocolate and fruit

Winter

Tea and coffee throughout the day.

Breakfast

Scrambled egg on toast

Two eggs and a piece of home-made bread

Lunch

Frozen home-made soup and 'posh' home-made bread

Evening

Seitan strips with cauliflower mash made with butter

Chocolate and fruit

BREAD! AND FLOUR

The first thing I need to say about flour is be careful to buy really good quality flour. Wheat is one of the cheaper staples. It forms such a basic part of our diet that it's an absolute waste of calories to put nasty empty calories or toxic cheap flours into your diet. Our favourite is spelt flour, especially organic spelt flour available from Lidl. I'm sure other supermarkets carry similar lines. Spelt is generally better quality and less likely to be tainted by pesticides than the cheap wheat alternatives.

Once you can reliably make a good bread, you can play around and make your own luxury breads which will be a healthy and filling staple. The only time you need to avoid healthy home made bread is if you're on a carbohydrate restricted diet, otherwise go for it! We have a few ideas for healthy and reasonably frugal home made 'posh' sandwich fillings and toast toppers coming up. But first lets make a good bread.

We recommend you buy a bread maker if you can. Use the dough hook on a big mixer if you don't have a bread maker. Note for frugalists: bread makers often turn up second hand and barely used because people follow the instructions on them which don't always produce a reliably good loaf. If you enjoy a good kneading session (or have anger issues!) note that you will have to put some effort in to mix as well without a bread maker. We *don't* bake in the bread maker because we find the results aren't as predictable and prefer a long large loaf.

Our basic bread mix

We use high gluten spelt (that's the strong white version). If you use any other than 'strong', add 5-10% by weight pure gluten. You can buy this online or at wholefood shops. It really does improve the texture, rising quality and protein value of your bread.

Recipe

500g flour, 7g salt and 7g dried yeast.

Add water slowly while mixing until it comes together into a ball. We won't give you a quantity of liquid because it can vary from country to country and humidity to humidity. Don't add too much with spelt, though, because it's completely unforgiving and your loaf will be sad and soggy. Ordinary white flour is more forgiving. We set the machine simply to 'dough' which kneads and rests a few times and also warms the mix to a consistent temperature. If you are hand kneading see if you can pull the mixture thin enough for it to be translucent without snapping. We are told this is a good test. It won't work on gluten free flour, though.

Now to rise. We don't double rise. We think that's too technical and can be tricky and unsuccessful.

Take your well kneaded mix and roll it into a nice loaf shape. Usually by tucking the edges under. Drop it into a 1lb loaf tin or onto a baking tray for a cottage loaf shape.

Leave to rise in a warm place (not too hot) until it doubles in size or just a bit more. Don't push it too far, though, or it will sag. If you like a slightly sour dough taste leave in a cooler place for a longer time or even overnight. Keep it in a greased bowl with a cling film top. Don't knock back, just carefully roll into the tin and bake immediately. Bake at 200c for 30-35 minutes. We leave a tiny tin of water in the bottom of the oven which seems to keep the bread moister and the crust crisper.

Tomato Bread

Add *two tablespoons of olive oil and 400ml of passata* instead of the water to the basic bread recipe, then add extra flour until your bread 'balls' as above.

Onion, turmeric and black pepper bread

Add *two tablespoons of turmeric and two of olive oil* to the basic bread recipe, *a quarter teaspoon each of ground cumin and coriander and 1/8th teaspoon of ground chilli powder.*

Chop one *very large onion* (or two medium or three smaller onions). I don't like to skimp on the onion flavour in this mix. Fry in a large flat frying pan in a knob of butter and a splash of olive oil (or cooking oil). Keep spreading the onions on the bottom of the pan and then turning them and spreading again on a high temperature at first and then turn down. We want to turn the onions golden but not brown. Add a good quantity of black pepper to taste. Leave them to cool and start the bread mix. If you are using a bread maker, wait for the final ingredient 'beep' and quickly add the cooled onions and a large pinch of salt. You will need to add more flour to get the onions mixing in rather than sliding around the outside.

Milk bread

50% whole-wheat 30% rye and 10% barley or oat flour and 10% gluten, 2 tablespoons of olive oil, salt and yeast as above.

Mix as above but use milk and not water. UHT full fat is fine and cheap!

Naan bread

Flour, yeast, salt and olive oil as above.

Small pot of Greek yogurt, plus water if you need any to make the ball.

Rise, cut into lumps, flatten into shape and throw on a hot flat pan. Turn when it's bubbly and has started to brown on one side. You'll see the surface change colour slightly when its ready to flip.

Chapatis

Chapati flour, water.

These are the easiest type of bread of all to make. I advise buying specialist chapati flour from an Indian and continental style store its cheaper that way. You know you're getting a great product for the job. Failing that white spelt is fine. You simply mix the water in until you get that nice bread ball as above and divide off a golf ball size piece for each chapati. Squish the edges of the ball into a flying saucer shape and drop on a floury surface. Flour your rolling pin well. Make one quick roll over the ball before slapping your hand down hard on to the dough. Twisting your hand so that the dough turns. Repeat this roll and turn over and over until you get a nice flat floury disc. Pick up the flat bread onto the palm of your hand and slap it down onto a hot flat pan. If you are lucky enough to have a chapati pan and a gas stove you can make them like a professional chapati maker. First flip the chapati over as it starts to change colour. Then after a few seconds you can flick the chapati over the edge of the pan straight over the gas flame. It will magically blow up. Pull it back and do the other side. You may need to use a tea towel to stop your hands from burning. And be very careful!

Incidentally, curry is a very frugal way to batch cook cheaper meat or lentils and tastes even better the next day. What better reason to try making chapatis.

Leftovers

Rediscover old favourites like bread and butter pudding, and making home made breadcrumbs.

I recently made three types of breadcrumbs. One of the ladies begging outside Lidl had gone by the time I brought out the pack of bread which she'd asked for. I was left with a bread I wouldn't normally eat in large quantities. But I hate wasting. I halved the baguettes and dried them out above my stove. Then I blitzed some up with dried garlic and some parsley the local veg stall just hands out for free and which I'd dried. The second mix was parmesan and onion which will make a nice crumb coating for bakes and the third a sage and onion, which I might use for stuffing. Since I have a problem with too much cheap white wheat, I'm more likely to coat chicken in it. All the mixes also had salt in, and they will keep for long enough in jars that I have time to come up with some recipes! But do make sure your bread is fully dry before blitzing and packing or you will end up with jars of mouldy bread.

RICE AND OTHER GRAINS

For boiled rice honestly, a rice cooker is a godsend! Keep an eye out for them in Lidl or Aldi or in charity shops. People don't often use them because they get out of the habit of cooking rice at home. Takeaways so often come with rice and it seems difficult to get right at home. A rice cooker makes rice right every time. And rice is a cheap base and just a little less carb-dense than potatoes. But still really nice and satisfying. If you are really struggling to find something to eat just cook up some rice and then add peas and anything else you like. Chopped up ham or frankfurter sausages are nice if you aren't vegetarian. Then run an egg and a splash of oil through it while its still cooking or in a frying pan afterwards.

Be careful with left over rice as it can develop toxins which can be very unpleasant indeed. You can keep home cooked rice in the fridge for a day but I wouldn't save it any longer than that. Don't save takeaway rice leftovers.

Risotto

Our favourite rice dish is risotto. I like it best when my husband makes it the long way standing stirring it for an age but it is perfectly nice made in a robot food processor. Just a little bit more 'gloopy'. Next time we try it I think we'll only set the stirrer for part of the cooking time.

Grain substitutions

Don't forget you can swap grains around and some of the harder grains are more nutrient-dense but need a much longer cooking time. Its worth experimenting.

Spelt risotto is absolutely wonderful. We accidentally ordered spelt grain instead of flour once and so were stuck with 5 kilos of the stuff.

We looked it up to see what we could do with it. It made a lovely nutty risotto and we couldn't get enough of it. Of course it took *much* longer to cook so if I did it again I'd use my slow cooker.

For a batch cook for freezer, or a party - it makes very economical meals

Spelt risotto base

NB. This is the base only. The main flavour is from the added ingredients, usually including butter, onion, garlic and whatever else you fancy.

1/2 kilo spelt (4 cups approx)

1 dessert spoon olive oil (enough to stir and coat the spelt while dry but not enough to cause 'foaming')

1 parsley and garlic cube

1 teaspoon mushroom powder (home made or bought).

Pinch of oregano

Pinch of thyme

Pinch of rosemary

Pinch of coriander seed powder

Pinch of paprika

Salt

Very slow cook 1.5 hours in rice cooker if you have one using the correct quantity of water for the cooker. Top up when required. Alternatively you can cook for several hours in a slow-cooker.

'Grain' puddings

Barley 'rice pudding' is also lovely.

Make milk puddings whenever milk is reduced or you have to use it up. You can use any type of milk but be careful because condensed milk is already packed with sugar. I wouldn't make it with too big a proportion of condensed milk unless you like it very sweet!

You can hard boil the barley in water. Drain it and put the grains into a slow cooker with lots of milk. (You can use the water to make lemon barley water if life gives you lemons!) You need around 4 times the milk to grain. You can add whatever flavourings you like in rice pudding. Cinnamon is good, cardamom, mace, allspice and vanilla if you have any. We got some tonka beans for Xmas one year. They're expensive, but a tiny scrape goes a long way. You'll need sugar of course but most recipes use much more sugar than I would. Since barley is a fairly hard grain, you can blitz it up if you want a softer pudding. Or semi blitz it leaving some grains for texture.

Tapioca pudding. Some kids don't like it because it can look like frogspawn. I love it, though.

Semolina pudding. Another old-fashioned milk pudding. Happy childhood memories again.

I'm not giving recipes for all these staples because you can find them all easily and you can also experiment yourself.

Tapioca in case you didn't know, is made from the root of the yucca. Yucca roots are regularly available in our supermarket in Spain and are an interesting, though more expensive potato substitute.

POTATOES

Potatoes are a great base for filling meals, and you will be able to get through a couple of hungry days using mostly potatoes, if that's all you have. But remember that they aren't much more than carbohydrates. That's no bad thing if you need energy, but don't imagine it's a full balanced diet. You will feel hungry a couple of hours after eating only potatoes so make sure you balance with some protein and vegetables if at all possible.

Here are some meals where potatoes are the star. Don't take any recipe for potatoes too seriously it's difficult to go far wrong.

Double cooked roast potatoes. Boil in water with rosemary and salt, Then either roast in oil and garlic until really crispy. Or you can deep fry. These are a favourite of ours but are quite naughty!

Baked. We microwave and then oven finish. My husband loves them with just vinegar salt and pepper but I need butter to make them edible.

New potatoes with minted frozen peas. A knob of butter on top makes this lovely even without any additions.

'Posh mash'. Just add loads of milk salt and black pepper and an obscene amount of butter and beat it into submission. Great if you've just scored some extra cheap butter on offer. Nice with sausages or a seitan dish. You don't need to overdo the meat if you make a lovely thick gravy. (I always save vegetable water for gravies).

Croquettes. Home made breadcrumb coating on mash with anything you fancy mixed in. Really they're just bubble and squeak with a continental name!

Spanish potato recipes to look up:

Tortilla de patatas. Just potato, onions and egg. Ignore any recipes that just look like a slightly fattened omelette. A proper tortilla de patatas should be at least 3 cm thick. And a fresh one is a delightful thing. If you ever have too many eggs, this is a really good use for them.

Papas a lo pobre. Spanish potato dish meaning 'poor man's potatoes' just contains potato, onion, green peppers and olive oil. A less poor man would add some Serrano ham pieces.

Wrinkled Canarian potatoes. New potatoes boiled and then slow roasted in their skins. They are served with a green or red 'moho' - another word for sauce.

CHEAPER FOOD HACK

Go semi-vegetarian! I can almost hear some readers shouting No! And suggesting all the way to vegan "never"! I'm not a vegetarian and certainly not vegan but I do believe that veggie food can and should be cheaper and conversely meat should be expensive. That's just a personal belief based on what I believe is sustainable. I'm just as annoyed by radical vegans as I am by radical carnivores but they do have a point. Meat is expensive to produce, and we are overly dependent on it. We don't need that much! Its a western disease to over eat meat and fish.

Learn to make wonderful vegetarian food and you will have a cheaper budget, it will be healthier overall and you can feel more virtuous about your effect on the planet and how many sentient critters you eat!

Seitan (vegetarian or vegan meat)

Seitan is a fantastic frugal food! The quantity of meat substitute you get is phenomenal for the cost. It is a vegetable protein, can replicate meat and can help prove whether you are really gluten intolerant, or if it's just modern wheats that affect you as they do me.

Because wheat gluten is so cheap (around £2.50 a half kilo) it makes a really good tight budget meat. Producing as it does about 1.7 kilos of 'meat' by the wet method so that makes it under £1.50 a kilo. Wow! That's cheap 'meat'.

Even adding butter to your meals)which I as a carnivore suggest to add back the moist fats a carnivore expects), it's still a very cheap protein base to your meals. There's no gristle and you know exactly what's in it. To me, in spaghetti bolognese for example, it's indistinguishable from mince. And I'm a born again carnivore!

You can also make stir fries or fajita wraps with strips of seitan, which doesn't suffer from being too chewy … although it does have a satisfying bite! This Christmas I bought my 'cheffy' husband a meat slicer from Lidl and he made kebab meat style fine slices which we served in pita bread with chopped up chard from the garden (still producing on Xmas day here in Spain) instead of lettuce, a creamy chive sauce with garlic chives, and a red salsa made with tomatoes, peppers and vinegar. It was absolutely delicious served on home made pita bread. We make seitan burgers by mincing with onion and using breadcrumbs and an egg to bind. We've been told by carnivores that these are just as nice if not nicer than their meat counterparts. You need a mincer (or mini food processor) for these recipes but Iwould argue that good kitchen equipment makes it easier to be frugal.

REGIONAL AND SEASONAL

The cheapest and most nutritious foods at any one time are those that are regional and seasonal. The very best places to find those are the local market if you have one. If you're a supermarket shopper, you can just rely on what happens to be cheap. Some supermarkets are now doing extremely cheap veg boxes of ugly and excess production veg (and fruits) and if yours has this offer get them. You can't choose what's in them. You can be sure that the items in the box are whatever is cheap in the supply chain at that moment. That's likely to mean it's at least seasonal if not also regional. Be prepared to work with what you get and if your store cupboard is well stocked with basics the challenge should excite you.

Its very natural, the most natural thing in the world in fact, for us to want to eat the same thing over and over and over. Until we're hugely sick of it. Then we find something else to love. Why do we resist that, and talk about balanced eating while trying to force ourselves into eating foods that are neither in season, nor nutritious? If such great variety was so important to us, the human race would only have survived in places where it could be obtained year round. If you eat from the garden, you need to eat less to get your fill of the nutrients you need anyway. And by the time the grapes ripen your mouth is watering to stock up on their sweet juicy loveliness. We always say (my husband and I) that there's a 'gazpacho day'. There is one day a year when suddenly the unappetising cold soup suddenly becomes the nectar of gods. Three months later and just as suddenly comes the day we would pass it on the supermarket shelves without a second look. You don't get that with other cold drinks so its not just the temperature and wetness, although that is clearly part of it.

Also, there is nectarine day. The day when all the supermarkets stock nectarines at just over one euro a kilo. Those nectarines are, after a couple of days ripening in the house, dripping with juice and delightful. Four weeks later the price goes up and they never ripen, going straight from hard … to wrinkly hard with not a drop of juice to be had. When you've lived a few years in a place, you learn the rhythm of the seasons both in the garden and the supermarket. You learn to love the gluts. You learn to buy the nectarines at one Euro 29 and leave them on the shelves when they go up to 1.45. You learn to bottle the things you can't live without (tomatoes usually) and you learn not to be interested in the others for the rest of the year.

There are fresh salad days and hearty soup days. Even the most hardened Tesco Metro shopping city dweller can learn the difference. We can all spot when the prices rise and fall. We can all go home with an armful of asparagus when it hits a pound (or a Euro) a bundle and enjoy it fresh with poached eggs or home made hollandaise. We whizz it up into a delicious freezable soup.

OUR IN SEASON GLUTS: VEGETABLE SPAGHETTI RECIPES.

Some vegetables give you two for the price of one. The vegetable spaghetti (sometimes called the spaghetti squash) starts by producing a short courgette which is delicious used as you would a courgette (zucchini). Then, when it's passed a certain stage you leave the fruits alone. They will swell just like a marrow into a big fat beautiful green and white striped and flecked squash. Cut it and take it into your pantry and use its beautiful golden strings to make a huge variety of recipes throughout winter.

We had a huge glut of spaghetti squash this year, and they keep very well throughout the winter. I've learned to love its frugal versatility and have included a good handful of quite different recipes for you to try.

Spaghetti squash is one of the most versatile winter squashes you can grow or buy. The colourful strings even make a pretty tasty mildly crunchy salad. Try these recipes on your family and see if they notice you're serving the same ingredient over and over again!

Don't forget you can also roast the seeds like pumpkin seeds. Lay them out on a baking tray and add a generous quantity of salt. Roast them in the top of your oven while you're cooking the rest of your pumpkin! The salt mostly gets on your fingers to flavour them when you're eating them just like ordinary pumpkin or sunflower seeds. The seeds are also fun for children to colour and thread.

Preparation of the squash

Preheat the oven to 220°C / 425°F. Cut the squash in half and scoop out the seeds and the very stringy seed surrounds.

Drizzle the squash flesh with olive oil and season with salt and pepper (no seasoning or oil for sweet dishes). Place cut side down on a parchment-lined baking sheet. Roast until the squash is tender when pierced with a knife, about 45 minutes to 1 hour depending on the size of your squash.

Author's spaghetti squash seitan bolognese

A cup of minced seitan. The sauce is made from chopped onion, celery salt or chopped celery plus salt, a spoon of mushroom powder, half a cup red wine and half jar of passata or a tin of chopped tomatoes (triturado in Spain).

Fry the dry ingredients then add wine and reduce. Add tomatoes, put the lid on lid on and bubble gently for half an hour. Serve over veggie spaghetti tossed in butter or oil.

Spaghetti squash fritters

1 medium spaghetti squash

Whatever cheese you like and have available! A mix of fresh and hard cheeses is good.

Zest of one lemon

Two tablespoons chopped fresh herbs (basil, rosemary and thyme)

1 medium clove garlic, minced

salt and freshly ground black pepper

One large egg, lightly beaten

70g or 1/2 cup flour

60ml or 1/4 cup olive oil

Mix 2 cups spaghetti squash, cheese, lemon zest, herbs, garlic, salt, pepper, egg, and flour. Plus breadcrumbs if liked. Stir until the mixture is well-combined – it should be thick and creamy.

When your frying pan is hot, add two tablespoons olive oil. Once the oil is hot, drop spoonfuls of the batter into the pan and cook until golden brown (3-5 minutes), then turn over. Be careful that your pan is not too hot or the fritters will cook too quickly on the outside and scorch before the inside is cooked. Serve with red sauce.

Spaghetti squash bake

Broccoli florets chopped into bite size pieces. 1 tablespoon of sunflower oil. 1 pre roasted large whole spaghetti squash. 6 ounces of plain greek yogurt. 50g or 1/2 cup vintage Cheddar cheese - shredded. 50g or 1/2 cup Gruyère cheese - shredded, 1 Egg - beaten, 1 teaspoon garlic powder or two cloves of fresh garlic, and salt and pepper to taste.

Preheat oven to 190°C / 375°F and grease a large casserole dish.

Dry your squash, if it's too wet, on kitchen paper. Remove the towel from the bowl and then add the yogurt, cheese, egg and seasoning. Add precooked broccoli, mix together and then pour the mixture into the greased casserole dish. Bake for 40 minutes. Of course you can replace the cheese for vegan cheese of your choice.

Spaghetti squash instead of pastry as a tart base. Brilliant idea!

Scrape out the spaghetti squash and press firmly into a greased tart former. Brush the tart base with oil and bake. Add quiche mix and bake. You can make a sweet version with unsalted squash and add lemon curd or custard for lovely sweet tarts. Ooh yum!

Caramelized onion spaghetti squash

While the squash is roasting, you should make the caramelized onion mixture. Onions are sautéed with butter and olive oil, rosemary mixed with kale, or broccoli if you can't get kale, and mushrooms for a healthy, colourful meal. You can add cheese too if liked.

Authors own 'sunny squash' sweet (because its so bright yellow).

Roast the squash without salt and pepper or olive oil. Mash the flesh with lots of grated ginger, honey, and a squeeze of lemon (juice and rind). Serve with custard. I just love this. Its easy to make into quenelles. Make it up to your taste. I'm a low sugar lover at the moment. If you want to add flour and make into fritters that would work really well too. Cost is just pence a serving.

I've also used spaghetti squash with potato 50/50 for lovely crisp tasty rosti.

LEAVE IT OUT, REPLACE IT OR MAKE IT YOURSELF

You'd be surprised how many expensive ingredients you can replace or simply leave out of recipes completely. For example my husband (the chef of the house) rarely bothers with white wine in risotto these days. If you're desperate for the acidity, just put a squirt of lemon or a dribble of rice or apple vinegar in.

We've never bothered to put the very expensive pine nuts in pesto, and it seems to make no difference. In fact we leave out the cheese too and just add it if we have it. Our basil is preserved by chopping in oil and salt and black pepper then simply freezing in balls or half-ball shapes in a silicone (pop) former.

Tahini in hummus. You have to balance it so finely to get it nice that we just don't bother at all and add chillis and lemon juice and red peppers, etc. instead.

You can also add Greek yogurt to hummus to make it creamier.

Cows milk is unnecessary in custard, breakfast cereal and coffee. You can replace all these with coconut milk. Its not cheaper but if you don't have milk in because you're trying to keep the shopping trips down I think its tasty and semi sweet and great for a lower-carb diet especially if you replace the custard powder in custard with egg yolks! You can use tinned coconut milk thinned 50/50 with water but don't get the low-fat one. The fat is the best bit! You can also use coconut milk to add a touch of luxury to a coffee made with one of the grain-based milks around.

Home made milk alternatives

I used to drink too much milk and was often told that cows' milk, because it was intended to feed fast growing baby cows, could also favour fast growing cancers. Whether you believe this or not there are also a lot of reasons to try alternatives and this doesn't mean you have to give up cows' milk altogether. My husband and I have discovered a liking for coffee made with a mixture of 80% spelt milk and 20% (full cream) coconut milk. Actually my husband likes slightly more coconut milk. The coconut milk is the more expensive part of it, but it does make it creamy gorgeous and is still a lot cheaper than going out for a coffee. The whole tin of coconut milk can cost less than the price of one coffee even in Spain!

Put a cup of rolled oats or rolled spelt into your blender with a litre of water, blitz for around 45 seconds (no longer than one minute) and sieve through a muslin cloth. Bottle and will keep for up 5 days. I'm told if you over blend or try to use flour, you get a slimy mix. That doesn't sound nice!

Home made multi-purpose flavour enhancers.

Mushroom ketchup (Derek's)

Yes, it works! And it keeps, according to my brother who is a bit of a forager and a lot of a foodie. "Best made with overripe field mushrooms but I often add ceps (boletus or porcini) if I have plenty of big ones. I got the recipe idea from a 1927 book called "The old master cookbook" by A Bonnet-Laird. Basically, you just chop up the mushrooms fine & layer with loads of salt, which draws out the liquor. Then you strain it off, boil it up with loads of spices, etc. and make the nearest thing to Worcester Sauce that you can and bottle it. It keeps fine 'cos of the salt content and is one of the best Umami sauces you can add to soups, stews, etc."

Dry mushrooms

My husband and I dry old mushrooms. Actually our fridge seems to do it for us as long as they aren't wrapped in plastic. In summer we just leave the half dry ones on a shelf to dry further. In the UK you can put them in a warm dry place or even dry them slowly in or on an oven or stove. I'd love a food dehydrator, but that would be a real luxury!

When they are fully dry to a crispy state, we just blitz them up in a mini blender. We put the powder in jars and it's a really good multi-purpose flavour enhancer for vegetarian food. When I asked my husband what he wanted me to buy him as a treat after he'd taken a horrible job off my shoulders, he asked for a big bag of dried boletus (ceps, porcini). It was expensive, but it will last for a couple of years and makes him a very happy vegetarian!

Dried fruit / peel / skin flavour powders.

Try dehydrating and powdering any of your favourite fruit gluts as a flavour enhancer or decoration. Raspberry is fantastic and zingy but expensive. If you have unwaxed oranges and lemons, peel off the zest and dehydrate. Then blitz to a powder. And I've been told tomato skins make an excellent flavour powder too. A little goes a long way. Always make sure your fruit is organic otherwise pesticides can be concentrated in the skins.

POSH FOOD, CHEAPER

Food which becomes fashionable is often just really good cheap ingredients prepared and cooked in the most delicious way possible.

So get cheffy! Chefs find the very best flavours in cheaper ingredients in order to maximise their profits. This is how they historically made poor man's food fashionable. In the past only the poor ate oysters. And before samphire became so fashionable we used to collect it on the shores of the river Humber. So If you can get hold of the same cheap ingredients you can have amazing food on the cheap and live like a millionaire frugally!

Basic black olive tapenade

This real favourite of mine has a very truffly flavour and can be served on toast, or with crackers or breadsticks, crackers or an addition to pizzas or pastas. It can also make a smear for meat dishes before cooking, or a spoonful adds flavour in a slow-cooked stew.

Tin of stoned olives and a little of the liquid.

Splash of olive oil

1 clove garlic

Squeeze of lemon

Black Pepper

Mushroom powder

Herbs to taste if liked, such as basil, chives, thyme, chilli extra salt if needed.

Blend. And put in a small jar with a layer of olive oil to aid preservation.

Basic Green olive tapenade

Very similar recipe as above but no mushroom powder. Has a fresher more acidic taste. Try to source olives without anchovy flavour so that its OK for vegetarians.

Tin of stoned green olives

1 clove garlic

Squeeze of lemon

Olive oil

Salt and pepper

Capers and/or coriander / cilantro leaf if available and liked.

Total cost, if you buy the olives on offer (75p to one pound a tin), around one pound fifty for a small jar full. Covers around 15 pieces of toast generously or 30 frugally. It tastes better after a day or two.

'Crab meat' alternative.

This fabulous recipe is from my Spanish friend Inma

It really tastes like the real thing and this recipe makes loads. So you can freeze or share or make for a party!

200 grams of seafood sticks. 1 can of natural cockles. 1 can of natural mussels. If you can only find pickled mussels rinse them or use frozen mussels. We get frozen mussels in Lidl here in Spain. *2 hard boiled eggs around 5 tablespoons mayonnaise* - to taste If you want you can put a glug of cream or a spoon of greek yogurt in the mix as well or instead. It depends if you want it to taste like unmixed down crab or a crab pate. If you remove the mayo add some lemon juice. Just blend them all with a stick blender for a smooth mix or mash with a fork for something more chunky.

Fresh 'posh' broad bean pate

This is fab! But it takes some time. If you have broad beans in the garden or can get the baby ones from the freezer at your supermarket. The younger the beans the lighter the flavour.

Boil the fresh broad beans in a little water until soft and the skins will come away. Around 10 mins.

Peel off the skins (You don't need to peel frozen baby broad beans). Mash with good glug of cream, UHT cream is fine for this recipe. We get UHT cream here in small cartons at 50-75 cents. A splash of lemon juice and lots of black pepper and salt. This will freeze in portion sizes in large ice cube trays or, better still, silicone mould shapes.

DIETING ON A BUDGET

Strangely you'll find in this section I don't have any recipes for diet food nor suggestions of pre-prepared diet foods to buy! That is because most of the recipes in the food section of this book are already healthy and good for maintaining a healthy weight. Here are just a couple of suggestions for dropping a few kilos reasonably quickly and more importantly some suggestions for treats so you don't feel deprived. Feeling deprived is the cause of most of our bad habits in life and especially in our diet.

Diet food is expensive. Don't use it. You don't need it and it's generally rubbish up-sold with the label 'diet' on it. It may have a lot of the calories removed, or they may even have replaced fat for sugar (a bad idea anyway) but it will generally just be low nutrition rubbish with a few vitamins and maybe some protein added.

When I was fast-dieting in preparation for a big operation after a smaller one where I'd lost a lot of blood, I needed to diet for the op. I also needed to keep up the nutrient levels in order to 'grow new blood'. And I wanted to strengthen my immune system. I was also trying to give up sugar because sugar is fairly widely recognised as being a food that cancer feeds on. Of course it was also one of the reasons my weight had climbed steadily since my mid 30s to 95 kilos / 210 lbs meaning I had been in the high 'obese' category for well over a decade. I was a sugar addict! I had to go pretty much 'cold-turkey'. I gave up the whole packets of biscuits and whole bars of chocolate and crisps and initially all carby foods like rice and wheat. (I added the rice and wheat back in moderation as I went below 70 Kilos / 155 lbs).

Of course it's easier when it's a life or death decision. Anything I could do to help my surgery to have a successful outcome, I was prepared to do. I was also very lucky that my husband had been told at the same time that if he didn't stabilise his weight and diet his health would suffer. So we both had every reason to lose weight during this time when we were also on a severely restricted income.

Here are a few ideas from my experience for a really healthy 'diet' which won't make you feel deprived.

Firstly remember fat is not the enemy. Always have butter and olive oil in the house. It will form a basis for most of your satisfying but low-carb meals. And will make those that have a few carbs but low sugar taste really good. Whatever you were told from the eighties until very recently, eating fat does not give you high cholesterol. Sugar does.

Eggs! Eggs are one of the finest sources of protein and a complex set of other nutrients you can get your hands on. They became one of the principle foods in my cold turkey transformation along with tinned coconut milk and red berries. Whenever I felt deprived I made custard from egg yolks and coconut milk. Dropping from a teaspoon of sugar to half a teaspoon finally to none. When you first try it it seems a bit short of sweetness but you soon start to taste the sweetness from the coconut milk. At first the coconut milk tastes a bit strange but after a while its cow's milk that seems strange.

If tinned coconut milk seems expensive if you're on a budget, look at it in the light of its nutritional value and it suddenly looks like a good deal. And paid for by that packet of custard cream biscuits you just put back on the shelf its a positive bargain!

My breakfast each day was eggs too. Bacon and egg, omelette or scrambled eggs. Yes, I admit I got a bit sick of eggs, but it was so successful that it was worth the discipline! My sister who has real trouble dieting but really tries, cannot get her head round the eggy breakfast idea because she says she "can't give up toast for breakfast". You have to remember that if you're working hard at a diet and still failing, that 'the thing you can't give up' is the thing that's holding you back. That old saying "if you always do what you've always done, then you'll always get what you always got" was never truer than it is with dieting. But you do need to remember to balance all these eggs with lots of healthy, fibre-filled vegetables and fruits. The weight simply dropped off me. And yet I felt better than ever. Not weak, tired or deprived. There was I recovering from a major operation feeling better than ever! I did have some pretty nasty off-days with the chemo but when they had passed I was feeling good.

I tightened up all this new looseness by walking. A lot. What's more at my husband's next blood test he was told all the warning 'stars' had gone from his chart and he could live to 108!

Buy organic versions of your staple foods if you can afford them. Although I realise this looks like an extravagance in a book about living on less, but you're eating so much less on your diet that the extra cost can be balanced out. You can even find you're spending much less but eating better. Your body craves more food if the food you do give it is low in nutrients. Conversely high nutrient foods calm the cravings and eating eggs can kill the cravings altogether!

As you start to add the carbs back use smaller portions of them and larger portions of veggies and protein to satisfy you.

So, my best dieting advice is about treats!

The one pudding a week rule

During the severe dieting phase, you can have a fruit 'pudding' with egg custard every day at lunch time, but it has to have no sugar at all or only a half teaspoon.

When I added wheat back (only organic spelt and oat flour for me as cheap wheat gives me headaches) I started to allow myself one pudding a week. Actually that pudding would last 2 days if I ate half of it which is more than enough!

My pudding recipe

One egg. A cup / 130g of mixed spelt and oat flour, a quarter of a teaspoon of baking powder, approx 50g lump of butter (I know that sounds like a lot but its lovely … and you take most of the sugar out so you have to have something!) *and one teaspoon of sugar.* Soften the butter and mix the rest of the ingredients in. Whisk it together with a fork or beat with a wooden spoon to aerate it until the mixture changes to a slightly lighter colour. If you need a little dribble of milk to soften it that's fine. "Its hard work" I hear you cry. Good! A bit of exercise will help you feel you've earned your treat! Bake the pudding in a greased dish for 20 minutes on a moderate heat. At first you'll say this is a tasteless mix. Don't worry you're putting it on top of red fruits and pouring custard all over it. No added sugar in the fruits though and only half to one teaspoon in the custard. Now I'm so used to this I sometimes even forget the sugar in the custard. The custard is made with eggs and whole coconut milk as above. You can use custard powder with coconut milk and some water if you're back on limited carbs.

THINKING ABOUT YOUR OVERALL BUDGET AND INCOME IN A WHOLISTIC WAY

Can I afford to change my life, do I want to change my life, what more do I want and what less do I want? What can I swap for more time? What would I be prepared to swap for more money?

The idea of living better for less is not a new one but many books or blogs or sites provide only one solution. 'Their solution'. The one the author chose for their own reasons. It was brought home to me very starkly back in my early days here when I still messed around with Spanish expat chat forums. Some people said that what we were doing "doesn't sound like living the dream to me". Not only were their dreams not achievable for me, but I'm not sure they were really that fulfilling. Although I think there aren't many people who wouldn't fancy trying sipping champagne on a yacht for a week or three. But how long would it keep its shine? And for proof of this, there were a number of people on the chat forums looking for and sharing information. Others spent their time just sniping at those who needed help. The snipers were clearly bored! For me, luxurious boredom might never be possible, but I'm unsure if those grumpy snipers really enjoy it. But let's for a moment make the assumption that you're reading this book because you want to look at the way you spend your money and your time for one reason or another.

Now let's look again at a subject more important than money. Time. Time is the most important commodity in the world and its the one thing which, at the end of the day, money just can't buy. It can buy your time working for somebody else. Or it can buy someone else's work for you and how we value our own time may be quite different from how we value someone else's. It's much more to do with how *they* value their time and their skills. So you may have to work three hours to pay your mechanic for one of his hours.

Say you work a 40-hour week, it used to be reasonable to expect that one-third of your income went towards housing, one-third towards utilities and one-third towards food and other needed and luxury items. Things have changed somewhat in the last 50 years and now those figures no longer apply so strictly. We all now expect luxuries to be cheaper, food to be cheaper, whereas housing seems in many places to have gone, pardon the term, 'through the roof'. Now there are other items not deemed to be luxuries any more but necessities. Transport, smartphones, tablets, the internet and annual holidays abroad.

Still, If you want to get the best out of your life and of your money / time balance, you do have to look at everything in terms of the hours of your day you are prepared to give them. In this way we will finally realise that our family time is one of the most expensive luxuries of all! But now we know its a luxury, perhaps we may value it more.

How much money does that extra hour at work give you? How much pleasure does going to the gym give you? What are the happy smiles of your children or of your ageing parents worth?

It's worth thinking about these questions before its too late and your kids have grown and gone.

What about time spent at the seaside or going for walks? Do you enjoy that or do you prefer TV and a bottle of wine? Chatting or arguing on the internet? Or a bit of everything? Only you know how many hours you need to work and at what income, to buy you the life you want. Do you want that life now or are you going to double or quits gamble it? This is your choice and yours alone. Sometimes when we're short of money, we feel strictured and lacking choice but being more frugal and a bit more aware of your work life balance can make you freer again.

WORKING LIFE PLANNING AND TOP UP INCOMES

You may wish to skip this section if you have your life all mapped out in front of you. Remember, though, things can and do change and when you least expect them. Having a certain bouncy flexibility and contingency plans B or C are often a good idea. If you have a job in the civil service, or as a teacher or doctor you may feel secure. If you can afford and have got a comprehensive insurance to cover life's unexpected slings and arrows. Most of us however these days are at the whims of those awful things 'market forces' and mechanisation. Sudden unexpected illnesses or bereavements just happen. Some may want to take time out from work to bring up children. In this case both partners may want to share the time off from a normal working week. Or would you rather take time off together? You need to look at what income you're going to need to make this possible. Some of us have only basic education or suffer from poor mental or physical health or may be prone to do so. In these cases its a very good idea to plan. I can tell you I never was an expert in this until recently. My world came crashing down because of an unexpected serious illness. I was living in a country which didn't cover my living costs for periods of sickness. I was ex-self-employed and ex-contract employed. Although luckily I was covered by their social security for my treatment. There was no sickness benefit, a situation which looks increasingly likely in Britain. I lived a whole year on what for most people would be virtually starvation income. I had a little help from family and friends for a very short time, and a lot of hard work as soon as we were both able to get on our feet again. It left me absolutely certain that unless you have a job and a works pension for life, you really need to be ready for a more frugal life and ready to change your working plans.

So, what did my experience as a self-employed person, along with my own crisis teach me?

Having multiple small incomes is safer than having one big income. That having lots of small but reliable trickles added up to one pretty reliable monthly stream.

Earning a lot less made paying tax simple. Immediately after my illness and until this year I was investing my time into many of the above. I just didn't earn enough to pay and therefore didn't have to declare my income every 3 months, just at the end of the year. Its worth thinking about whether you can or whether you want to stay under this threshold. It is superfrugal level and not for everyone. This year I will probably earn over that level and begin to have to pay.

There's a difference between earned and unearned income and royalties, etc. come into the latter. I'm still trying to work out what this means to me.

Some ideas for small income streams

Part time work

Small internet sales: Ebay, Etsy etc.

Direct website sales

Royalties on artistic output. Photographs, illustrations, books, artwork, Youtube etc.

Youtube is now known to pay a pittance compared to other output. It is only worth considering if you have something you think will go viral or something which will advertise your other products.

Mine is now a multiple small income stream approach comprising some irregular incomes like teaching which is small lumps every now and then. I write craft and other books and am adding more to my inventory. I sell about 60 books a month currently. We aim to earn between 1.30 and 2 pounds a book. I'm getting over 100 a month so-called 'passive' income from them, and about 50 more from other royalties. I also, incidentally to my book writing, make things which I pass to my husband to sell. He runs the craft business. And I also have a page on Patreon.

If you're a creator of some kind with a following, you can start a Patreon page which is a bit like crowdfunding, but a regular monthly subscription where your fans support you, perhaps in return they get some exclusive access. This kind of thing builds slowly, so you have to invest just a little extra time each month setting up and managing your page but over a year or two you should be able to get enough of your fans to support you for enough dollars to make it worth your while. I have a Patreon page and its very affirming. Your Patrons support you because they know you need an income and you give them something back which they can't get anywhere else. It works to bring you a small but reliable income from sharing your art *and* in my case, it helps me with my self-discipline. You can also set up your own private subscription platform but its more difficult and time consuming to manage.

Selling tutorials via online education platforms - Skillshare, Teachable, Udemy etc.

Affiliate schemes - Amazon affiliate scheme etc. these work best if you've developed a following first with a blog, Youtube or your creative work.

Some of the above can lead you to anything from tiny to very large incomes indeed. A friend of mine got herself into a self-publishing niche market of which she was a leader. She made a nest egg that will carry her and her partner through to old age. But of course you can still hit the wall with an unpopular product you've invested a serious amount of time on. So keep your plans small and achievable and expect each to pay off over the longer term and not the shorter.

Private Teaching. One to one can pay up to 25 pounds an hour but small groups can get you 30 to 40.

There are other income streams if you are unemployed or semi employed but of course if your income is more than a scrap or bartered you will have to declare.

If your garden is producing more than you need you can sell eggs, vegetables or plants / seedlings / seeds.

You can buy and sell second hand or antique goods or be a car boot seller.

None of these will make you much money but its better than a kick in the teeth.

You may actually want to or have to be unemployed for a while if your mental or physical health is poor. If you can, do something. Work towards something. It can be whatever makes you happy. Just don't give in to despair because that is very damaging.

BANKS, DEBT AND PAYMENT PLANS

I'm not going to attempt to give you a lot of money advice. I'm simply not qualified.

I'm not a great fan of banks. They have done little for me except double my debt when I was unable to pay by using their swingeing 5 pounds a day unauthorised overdraft fees. These were over quite a period during their own crash … and mine, when there was not enough money to pay direct debits. Instead of refusing them they paid them out in order to excise their unfair daily charges. We had no recourse because the time taken to try and remove these unfair charges coincided with the time we psychologically needed to run away from the problem. Eventually, we got a Payment Plan sorted out but by that time our debts had doubled. I use banks now only when absolutely necessary. A lot of my income now comes through Paypal, but I do have bank accounts to spread the risk of frozen accounts, etc. which could cripple a business, and to pay for things where there is no ability to pay by Paypal.

Make sure you know what the charges are for. Make sure you dispute any unfair charges. Don't whatever you do bury your head in the sand like we did when things get out of hand. Go immediately to a charitable payment planning company such as Payplan for help. There are plans in which you can manage or avoid bankruptcy. Other debt help groups do exist but I was unable to find anyone who wanted to talk about their own experiences with debt management. N.B. Be careful. There are companies who advertise that they help with debt but exist only to convert your current debt into a more expensive loan. This may be appealing when you're desperate but only compound the problem and you could lose your home.

My husband uses our joint bank account to run the business. I do once again have a credit card which of course is a very useful piece of kit. There is a world of difference between not buying stuff because you don't need it and not buying it because you can't. Especially if you really do need it. One example is if you are self-employed and you can't afford a pack of printer paper or some postage. These things can crush your business and are the one time when I would rather use a credit card if I have access to one than crush my business. But the credit card is a slippery slope for the frugalist who doesn't have very strong self control or bends to pressure to go to that family reunion or pay for your share of a takeaway or example. You need to be super aware of that. So banks do have their uses, though I will never quite trust them again.

Heading for the sh*t!

So. You've reached as near as dammit rock bottom and you need to climb out. Like me you're an idiot with money and spend it whenever its there. Well, there's this old-fashioned thing called a piggy bank. It doesn't have to be a pig. Mine's actually a very nice little acorn. Well from tiny acorns … Anyway, mine can't be that small, although it looks like it because it actually holds ... well to be honest I don't know how much it holds but it's a lot more than you'd imagine. We actually lived for 3 weeks off the butter knife wranglings from that little acorn last summer. In the end I gave my husband 40 euros to pay a bill that had reached toxic. I religiously, even joyously dropped all my one-euro coins into the acorn even denying my husband the couple of euroquid he wanted to take to the market. I'd give him a fiver instead with a stern warning to bring something back for the acorn. Of course this meant as soon as I broke a note it was gone but that just made me more reluctant to break one. This may seem obvious and somewhat patronising, when you're on what we call 'the bones of your arse'. Really it's easier to feel the pinch to build up a tiny safety net now while you only have next to nothing, than it is to find you have absolutely nothing.

Once I'd got through that summer, I decided on a back up acorn. One was ongoing and became our emergency money. The other is now 'I'll open that when hell freezes over, or my daughter decides on a wedding date', whichever set of circumstances actually happens.

Check your mortgage repayments now you've become frugal.

www.moneysupermarket.com/mortgages/overpayment-calculator

on 100,000 mortgage at 5% interest rate over 25 years I calculated through this site that by making monthly overpayments of £150 … Your mortgage would be paid off 8 years and 2 months sooner than you would have otherwise. This would save you £25,967 in interest over the life of your mortgage.

That is significant. But so is finding that level of extra money.

MORE EARNING OR TIME POTENTIAL.

Do you want to downsize, or even earn more?

Do you want your creative output to be your main job or your backup? This may affect which jobs you choose for extra income. If you're a creator as your main job you might need a monthly pay check you can rely on. Bar work restaurant or night cleaning etc.

But there are other ways to achieve a small but adequate monthly income as a frugalist.

You need to do some maths and see how little you can live on and how much leeway you need for comfort.

My daughter and I were talking about her embryonic craft business. She currently has a full time which she enjoys and is efficient at. We chatted about the necessity of keeping it. Both agreed that when she has enough leverage to ask for a raise, she will propose to have reduced hours instead. A win-win for the company. Keeping an employee who can do really good work in short order and doesn't laze around for the rest of the week. She goes home and does the other things which make her happy and fulfilled, leading to her being more contented when she gets back to work.

How to make your work pay more than once

My biggest single tip is to get used to the stacked income idea of making sure that everything you do can have more than one use. That is to say each job can pay more than once. It works for planning your working life especially for planning what projects you take on. In my case my work can now produce two or even three incomes. Mostly you can do this if you're prepared to publish. Within a few years of starting my crafts business, I was asked to teach my pretty innovative ideas. Fortunately, my English level was OK (I can't say the same for my punctuation which continues to be appalling) and I could express myself fairly well and even write reasonably entertaining prose. So I developed, made, taught and wrote (and photographed) many of these processes concurrently. I was pretty sloppy about it in those days and not very business savvy, I just worked that way naturally. I'm always trying to find ways to do more for less effort. I'm just like my father before me, a hard working lazy person. In the past that was because I undervalued and underpriced my work so the extra concurrent income streams were important. So here are a few examples. I make my craft items in batches by techniques that allow me to make larger numbers at the same time. At the same time I often write those processes up as a 'how to' magazine project, which may go on to be part of a book. It takes a little longer to make but I get extra income out of it. Why? Because I then publish the project in a craft magazine, earning around 75 pounds a page. I have to say payments for articles have actually stayed stagnant in the past 20 years and could be less or nothing except free advertising. The reason for this is that magazine distribution is dwindling. I have been writing articles on and off for many years. The article would give away my new ideas and techniques for quite a low income but only if the readership liked them enough to copy them. They did. A slight minus on the balance sheet. *But* I didn't give copyright to the articles away. I insisted on keeping that for future books. I always did it this way because before I even started writing articles my first book was planned and approved. This turned out to be the best way to work. If you have ideas worth reading you can 'monetise' them over and over. That is to say sell them in many different ways and on different platforms. For example I use Youtube, and I share the newest ideas as they come up on Patreon with my best friends supporters and fans. I also continue to write articles, as the publicity value for the end of this chain of repeatable products, my books. I also intend to get into Skillshare. In addition to all this when all the writing photographing, filming, etc. is done I can sit and finish my own makes and, of course sell them online and at the fairs I attend. These days I sell them at nearer the right price. In the old days of course I didn't, which gave rise to this little old lady living frugally out of necessity.

How many artists or crafters do you know who have a pension plan? I do now of course and that is pretty much doing all of the above that I've learned to do, but doing it smarter. And of course doing them for as long as I'm able. No penthouse or holiday cruises but hopefully enough income as long as I can write … and a bit longer which brings me to the subject of long tail incomes.

The craft items I make sell well but cheaply. When they're gone, they're gone and the money dries up. But the money is quickly in your hand sometimes even in cash or barter. You can be left with no stock and no money during illness or a downturn in trade though.

Books and other educational platforms can fill that gap but only if you self-publish. I have a bit of a jaded view of publishers because often your contract can be corrupted in ways you didn't expect. Fortunately my contract was not so tight that I couldn't get out of it and we've had a fairly amicable 'divorce'. Although the publishers can sell 10 times as many books as I can, I get 10 times less in royalties and so the income is approximately equal from self published books. The upside is I don't get so many copies of my work for so little income. I'm actually better off this way and I decide if I want to recall, enhance, abridge, republish, translate etc. Much more freedom. I've only just realised what powerful tools these are. And I never have to worry about whether the publisher might decide to remainder my books. Or if they're ripping me off by rolling full price sales in with extreme discounts in order to pay out less. There are many other sneaky tricks some publishers get up to.

I've been trying to suggest for years that the key to unemployment and the pension crisis is a sliding scale of employment. This consists of the idea that youth should combine freedom with learning and employment. Some of that learning should come from mentoring schemes where they can access free skill-sharing from older people who are sliding back out of employment into a pension according to their physical and mental capacity for work. The older people should be paid for by a pre-pension plan if they have skills to share. And a universal basic income if they have not. In the absence of enlightened political thinking in this area, we can at least encourage this part of it ourselves and sell our skills at a low price per person to make up for a shortfall in employment and income. This is more tricky than I'd like to make it sound of course. As a society we lack confidence in ourselves as mentors if we don't have certificates to prove competence or its non-paper equivalent confidence. Yes, its easy for me to say. I've been teaching for years without ever setting foot in a school or university. (except when their halls were booked for events).

Teach anything you know. Per hour, per day, online or in person. In Spain particularly there is quite a culture of sending your kids to private lessons in order to help them get ahead. But adults want or need to learn too.

My language teaching happened organically but although I was nervous and made mistakes, I was no more or less afraid than a student teacher doing their first teaching practises. The most important thing is learning to value yourself and your skills and then pass them on with love and consideration in exchange for a small but reasonable amount of money per person per hour. Its easy and very effective to teach a class of 5 students at 5 pounds an hour each netting you a healthy 25 pounds an hour. A frugalist especially as part of a couple with basic needs can live off four hours a day of work at this rate. A healthy top up for another part time job or a pension top up could be 2 hours just 4 times a week. You need to remember you can't make a standing start at this level, and you will need to build up a reputation perhaps with smaller classes or one to one. If you're teaching young people you also need to make use of your piggy-bank since there are usually no classes in summer or Xmas. If your first reaction is "oh no I can't stand kids people or dogs", ask yourself if that's really true? I started teaching adults one-to-one and was sure I wouldn't enjoy teaching kids. I'd forgotten that I used to work in play schemes before my own children were born. My dislike was possibly a biologically imperative dislike of other peoples children as compared to my own! After a very short time these new little sparkly eyed naughty and excitable people morphed into being 'my own' in the sense that I became invested in their success. My motherly response had kicked in! Some days and sometimes you have to dig deep but that can be the case with your own children too.

Here are some of the skills you may have to share

Literacy and numeracy

Crafts

Art

Mathematics

History ,geography or science

Marketing

Computer literacy

DIY

A language

You may have a skill that you might not even have thought of. You may think you don't have the patience or the skills for teaching though. You'd be surprised. Its not easy at first but if you need the money and the parents need you, its win-win.

Here are some quickie tips for English teaching in Spain, which is one of my minor income streams. Or indeed Spanish teaching in England! Some of these tips also apply to teaching or cramming anything anywhere. You can charge 5 pounds or euros per child per hour and you can teach at home or in a hired building. One word of warning: strictly you need all sorts of permissions and stamped bits of paper. In a small village or neighbourhood, you simply need a good reputation and to care about doing a good job. Classes of 4-6 are ideal. Any more and you really have to be good at crowd control and not care about some kids getting lost along the way. I can't do that, nor would I, because I care about the value of the 'service' to both my kids and to my customers the parents. So I keep classes very small.

Be kind to the kids. They might not want extra lessons. Their lives are pretty tough anyway, and they're often overburdened with homework.

Be strict. Don't allow disrespect to yourself or between them. But be cheerful. Fast discipline and endless benevolence are needed.

And the most important one MAKE IT FUN.

If you're teaching a language, don't try to teach grammar at first. The chances are you won't really understand it yourself. Just be a play leader. Find opportunities for using English words and make a game out of it.

Teach the alphabet or words of songs using musical chairs.

Teach anything at all using movements. In, on, under, behind, (prepositions of place) using your hands and your two thumbs to point over your shoulder to behind yourself.

Repetitive word jokes with very young kids like pencil pencil pencil PEN (showing and hiding the two) to differentiate between two items or between two similar words as in Soup soup soup SOAP.

If you work at a language academy, you may have to accept lower take-home wages, but your boss may help you get your certificates and qualifications, and your income will be official and fully paid up for national insurance tax and the like. Plus you'll never have to take your payment in fire wood or horse manure both of which I've done! Actually I've really enjoyed being paid that way!

In order to help other busy people's children with literacy or numeracy, you don't have to be a mathematician or an English degree holder. You are only the foundation on which they will build. I truly believe that teaching a love of learning is more important than exactly what you teach.

So what about childminding? If all the above hasn't filled you with horror, how about passing whatever qualifications in childminding you need. There is a real dearth of good quality childminders, and parents will pay a premium for a childminder with all their certificates and ratings, etc. who offers something extra like a language or real pre-school development in a creative or scientific area. Don't get involved with parents who are pushy for pushy's sake. Those who really want their kids to learn the enjoyment of learning will make great customers and indeed partners in your enterprise. If you only want to work mornings … or afternoons … or evenings why not try to pair up with like-minded neighbours to provide a whole day service.

Yes, you can also walk dogs or house-sit for pet owners for accommodation, travel and a basic income. If you are in a rut ask yourself what you enjoy doing right now and see if there are steps between that and a bigger income for less work. Because you don't have to stay poor to be frugal!

VALUING YOUR TIME AS SELF EMPLOYED IN THE ARTS

How many people do you know who are salaried, who would say that they are earning far too much for what they do? Nobody, right? They would all defend their income level by explaining how hard the work is and how long the training; or how expensive the investment in their degree or masters or professorship. Everyone, including those who really enjoy their work. Everyone that is, except artists. A creator almost bows their head and squirms when they ask for their price, no matter what price that is. Very few have grasped the notion of the value of their work, even fewer take into account the value of their training and their knowledge. Even those who have learned their art by following others have invested in the books, the courses and the trial and error. Nothing done well is really ever easy. It might come easier to some to put that effort in. Some more easily learn from their mistakes, and most of us make art or work self-employed because we love it. Sadly, no matter how hard earned, we see being creative as a privilege and a gift and we allow others to see it that way too.

Think back into pre-history to the place of the artist in their society. I imagine that a gift for constructing pots or carving and engraving wood or stones or making clothing and jewelled pins was much more highly sought after. The creative was an integral part of society just as much as the farmer or the hunter. Later the decorative artist oiled the wheels of commerce producing the signs of wealth which every elder and then businessman craved. So, when did we decide to devalue the role of artisan? Perhaps it was then when those who created the signs of wealth along with everyone else became subservient to those who owned it. So how does the artist regain that sense of self-worth? I think by calculation. Are you now skilled in your craft? And are you aiming to be more skilled? Calculate how long your foundation course took. How long your 'degree' and how long your masters if you've got that far. If you didn't go into further education, how many years did you put part time into learning the skill you want to sell? How much has this time earning the minimum lost you in 'proper' wages. And ask yourself whether your skill level in what you do is as great as say a teacher, a banker, a lawyer. Don't ask yourself whether you enjoy the work, most people who have reached a high level in their work derive satisfaction from a job well done. Most of us have days when we really would rather not make that commission or deal with that customer. Most of us don't enjoy throwing yet another batch of something which didn't work into the bin. All of that is work. Bankers and accountants enjoy their work too. Some of them don't but the only reason they don't become artists is because of the low pay. And that … is our fault. Being an artist is a neo-liberal dream job. "Let the market decide". We can do that, but we have to tell the market what we expect and then the market will decide if we are worth it.

At the moment however, we are expecting too little. So, what should we be expecting? Well, I think with my level of expertise I should be expecting 40,000 a year in any other job. That's just over 25 an hour for every worked hour assuming I work a 37 hour week for all but 8 weeks of the year. And why not. This is my party after all. And remember I don't get any sick pay! So that's what I should aim for. Does that sound like the right way to think? If it does it then becomes much easier to value your time. If my husband were to aim for a similar amount, we'd be a lot more able to cope with the slings and arrows. But that's a ridiculously high expectation … isn't it? Well only until people "get it". After all JK Rowling was a struggling single parent at one time. Now of course we all know she's worth her money and no-one would question that nor envy her it since she pays her taxes and is humble enough. We do seem to demand a humility from artists which we don't expect from high financiers and other celebrities. So there's a figure to aim for. But do we go in expecting to get it immediately? Of course not. We're only at the beginning of revaluing ourselves. We have to go through the pain before the gain. One thing I've seen from artists who do make it: they make good art first, and the money follows them. The only difference between them and us is that they value their time correctly.

How much per hour do you need to earn to get from your current 10 thousand a year to 40. Well, it seems four times as much or more so it seems we need to up our prices to a level where only the very best of the very best will survive. We're going to have to think in terms of 'upping' our hourly rate from the national minimum which is what most artists currently 'award' themselves, to around 25 pounds an hour. Does this sound ridiculous and unworkable? Well its either this, or undervalue ourselves, or find other ways to make our work pay.

SPEND LESS, GET MORE

If you can get 30% off all your spending that could be translated as 30% off the hours you have to work to earn enough to live. There may be a slightly more complex formula, please forgive me for sweeping generalisations and suppositions. I'm neither an accountant nor an economist. But 30% off taxes you pay on that product has to make you feel good. If you could always get a 50% discount you could work part time instead of full time. And that brings down your tax to pay even further. Its as simple as that. If you can get 70% off it will balance the times you only get 30% off. Let me just say right here the point for me is not about tax avoidance because to me we should all happily pay our share of tax. But here are the important words. *Our share*. If we consume fewer resources and we give back to our society more in different ways such as being more ecologically sound. More plugged in to community action or more sharing of our talents it stands to reason that we owe less to society and we have less overstock of wealth.

Learn to barter and complain.

Membership and subscriptions top tip: always cancel free trials. Never allow them to run. You will see why below. Note the companies do make it as difficult as possible within the constraints of the law to find and cancel trials. Be persistent and set reminders so that you never forget to cancel a trial membership.

Sky

My son tells me every year about the great deal he got from Sky. Clearly they have more than one price. Let's face it; they have a service which costs you no more to send out to 11 people than to 10. They want to catch those extra customers and squeeze out that extra profit. You can be that extra customer. This only works if you are prepared to play hard ball and you are prepared to lose. If Sky channels are everything to you and you can't live without them then maybe don't try this. If you are that extra customer who can live without Sky but who would like it if its cheap enough this idea is for you. Be prepared to ring up and cancel your membership each year. When they ask you why, say you can't afford it. If they offer you a tiny discount say nope, still can't afford it. If you are then asked what would make you buy it, pick half-price and stick to it. If they say no just cancel anyway. The chances are they will get back to you within 3 months to offer you a great deal that you *can* afford.

Incidentally, one of my sweetest memories (as parents don't often get told that they were right) was when my son thanked me for teaching him the practice and art of complaining. When he was younger, he had always been excruciatingly embarrassed if his mum argued the toss about bad service or faulty products in front of him. Clearly he's now a chip off the old block and will no doubt embarrass his own children with it too. More about my son's complaining successes later.

Kindle and Kindle Unlimited

Reading is one of the pleasures, indeed necessities I advise for the interest education and mental health of any frugal person/family. I gave up reading when I first married because of the problem of reading in bed. Bedtime was the only time I've ever had time for, and therefore interest in, reading. When my kids bought me a Kindle-enabled tablet about 8 years ago I joyfully took it up again and haven't stopped since. I take up a Kindle Unlimited offer once a year or so just to hoover up the books which are on Unlimited. Then I cancel again after a month or two. When I've come to the end of the interesting stuff available and any new authors I want to check out, I cancel again. I then go back to buying fewer, but longer and often more educational books.

If you keep your Unlimited membership open, there is a law of diminishing returns. Don't forget to cancel when it goes up in price or when you've cleaned out the interesting books available in your favourite genres.

Amazon audible membership.

Here's another of those digital products where the seller needs to catch every last possible consumer. A lost consumer means no income at all from them. This is why you can often add the audiobook to your purchase of the digital (ebook) version for just a small additional cost. There are some books where its actually easier to listen than read and of course some people need to listen rather than read. I have to say right off the bat that the price of digital products is too high anyway especially if the paper version is lower than the digital version. I almost resolutely refuse to buy overpriced digital products. I was persuaded to try a free Audible promotion where you get a credit per month for nothing during the one-month trial and for 7.99 thereafter. After the trial, if I let it run, I was committing myself to paying 7.99 per book even though I could often get an audible add on to a Kindle book for just 2.99. So of course I set an alarm on my husband's tablet to remind me to cancel the membership. I shouldn't have been surprised of course when they offered me the next 3 months at half-price. If course I accepted. 3.99 is the right price for a book. In fact I have just purchased a 17.99 audiobook with my 3.99 credit. Quite a saving. Although as you'll imagine I would never have bought it at the top price. Incidentally check out the price of just getting the ebook version and then the add on. It may be hardly more expensive or even cheaper. Offers come up on digital books too. Resist over-pricing. There are lots more books to read while you are waiting for digital publishers to see the sense of dropping their prices.

By resolutely standing your ground against over-pricing of digital consumables, consumer stubbornness can pay off and could even cause something to be cheaper for the poorer members of society. How amazing would that be?

Insurance claims.

There are some people who claim every penny they can from home insurance etc. I'm not one of those but I wouldn't say I was right in this respect. Its certainly true to say that the more people who claim, the higher the premiums. My advice is claim if you need to. Unless of course its a claim for flooding because claiming may lower the value of your house. Only claim if everyone in your street are claiming in this case because your area's insurance is going to go up and house values will go down anyway. So you have nothing to lose. Of course if your losses are major, you will need to claim. That's what insurance is for!

Broken tech (especially American tech)

I'm not a claimer, and am too honest for my own good. So when the Fitbit my kids bought me for my Xmas present twanged off my wrist as I was undoing it, and hit my floor tiles at an unfortunate angle smacking and cracking the screen, my first thought was "my fault". Because of this I wrote a polite little email to the company asking them to provide me with the address of a repairer. They quickly replied telling me they had no repairers in my area and please accept 25% off a new device. The Fitbit cost well over 100 pounds at the time, and I was living at poverty level. Even though I was still thinking it was my fault it broke, this annoyed me a bit. I told them that I wasn't happy with their answer and I needed to get the item repaired . I reminded them that not all their customers could afford their expensive watches and that some were old skint ladies like me, who were given them by a loving family for health reasons. This time their reply was along the lines of "we are sorry that none of our solutions is acceptable to you". This reply woke up the justice warrior in me because I hadn't been offered solutions in the plural just the one "buy another one". I can't bear arrogance, especially in a rich person or company. So, after a day of musing and thinking maybe I'd lost this one, I wrote back. This time I reminded them that they were selling a sport watch with an elastic wristband. It was a wholly predictable situation that while taking the watch off it might 'ping' out of control and hit one of those hard floors. Yet they seemed to have saved money by not putting 'Gorilla-Glass' in their product and there was no warning to remove the watch in a certain way (by holding it against the body or over a towel for example). This combined with the total lack of any repair facility meant I had no option but to demand a replacement. Then I sent the email with a cc to BBC Watchdog knowing that the company would see that I had done so. Result: a return email promising me a new Fitbit which arrived a couple of weeks later. It pays to get righteously pissed off!

Bad holiday experiences

My son again is very careful when he buys a holiday. He does all the research and gets the Trip Advisor info. He had heard that a hotel he was taking his family to had had a bout of 'hand foot and mouth' disease. An illness that tends to affect children and is more distressing than dangerous. But he had read that it spoiled some people's holidays at that resort. So my son, ever diligent, got in touch with the holiday company and asked them if this problem had cleared up. They assured him that it had. Unfortunately, it hadn't, and both his children caught the disease. It did rather spoil the second half of their holiday. Although my son would be the first to say not completely. It was just a damper on their activities in the second half of the week. Having made the first contact he contacted the holiday company again and told them he was disappointed that this had happened to his kids despite their assurances. He was given rather a nice little cashback which did make up for the inconvenience.

Cheeky reselling of returned goods.

We bought a printer in Media-Markt which looked like the right price for the right product. When we got it home my husband set it up and printed out a status report including of the ink cartridges. We were shocked to see nearly 50% of the ink had been used already! We took it back of course and turned down an offer of a similar machine since we didn't much like the machine anyway. I don't know how that machine had come to have that much used toner. I can only think that someone had used and returned it. This is definitely one to watch out for since consumables are a large part of the expense of running printers. We chose a different brand with consumables available at a higher, and therefore cheaper capacity.

Printers again

On the subject of printers, watch out for the built-in obsolescence con! You will almost certainly at some time get a warning notice that your waste tub is full and needs replacing or and this I find really annoying that some other part is worn out. I can't even remember the different items that were supposedly in need of replacing on our old Samsung laser printer. Each time my husband has been to internet forums and found out the fix which is always simple. Often its a fuse that is set to blow at a certain time after the printer is first used (another reason to check yours isn't a return) or just a press of a switch. Until this is stamped out, *and it must be,* this practise is consigning heaps of old printers with perfectly serviceable parts to landfill.

www.ifixit.com offers repair info on many types of electronics and cars.

Don't fall for the consumables con either. You can buy the originals if you can afford them. Most people reading this book can't. There are always companies offering compatible cartridges at much lower cost. Very occasionally these cartridges won't work but the companies selling them *will* replace or refund. We have plenty of experience of this and have never had a refusal of a complaint. And these suppliers are often easier to contact and to deal with than the original company.

GIVING UP BAD AND EXPENSIVE HABITS

I think in order to crack any bad habit you need to work on the way you think about it. I really believe it works in exactly the same way for giving up all bad habits. I think first you have to work on the whole 'giving up' idea. Even the language is negative and reeks of deprivation, whereas the idea of giving yourself something, rewarding yourself, is what drives us really hard. Psychologically we are conditioned to want the feeling of reward which our parents gave us when we were good. We think that now we are adults we are in charge and can trigger that feeling whenever we want, and we do. But just like smoking or eating the reward loses its power and you have to have more and more of it to feel content, so we develop self-rewarding habits that become more and more deeply ingrained and just the idea of 'giving up' can make us feel anxious and bereft.

I've had pretty much every one of these addictions to a greater or lesser extent during my life. I never did have a drug habit but that's because I had a strong enough fear of that. I also had the fairly good idea that if I tried it … I might like it. Even though now almost free of all of them, I'm still working on a fairly compulsive craft hoarding habit! Of course I'm still an addict so those old compulsions still sit somewhere in my psyche, but they are more like old enemies that I don't trust back into my life than old friends: and I'm pretty comfortable not to let them back through the door.

My successes when I've had them in leaving behind bad habits have always centred around the idea that I wasn't giving up something but that I was giving myself something new. I could distil it down to just one word: Freedom. But of course its a little more complex and messy than that.

Smoking

I don't know where I finally got the ideas which helped me give up smoking thirty years ago, but I do know that it was important, to me at least, that I'd had a failed attempt first. A failure isn't so much a failure but an experience. This is a very good way to think about past attempts that happen before this last successful one. That 'failure' was obviously my first cigarette, and I knew that next time that was the one cigarette I couldn't have … The *only* one I couldn't have. The excuse I gave myself for succumbing to the temptation of that first cigarette was the very real and weird 'spacey' feeling the sudden loss of my drug of choice and the effects of a new drug ... oxygen was having on my body and mind. Once I realised that some people would pay a fortune to feel that 'spacey' and decided to welcome it as a free and legal 'high' I knew I stood a chance the next time.

Someone had also told me that it was a very good idea not to give up without a plan. And that plan was particularly setting a date far enough ahead in the first instance not to give me the 'heebie-jeebies' and send me running for another packet of 'fags' to counter the nervousness even the thought of giving up my 'prop' would cause. And so it was that around 6 months after my youngest child's birth and a couple of months after I gave up my then job through post natal depression I decided my first self-help task was to give up smoking again ... (for the second time) so I set the date a month or so later. My poor child had had to endure my nicotine habit in-utero and I felt guilty enough about that. I wasn't going to subject her to any more smoking. Her dad and I had already decided we wouldn't ever smoke in the same room as her.

My primary incentive for giving up was this wonderful newborn little girl and my two boys. In my mind it loomed very large that I was now 32 and my mother and grandmother had both had heart attacks, fatal and nearly fatal at the age of 42. One more decade with my children was definitely not enough! I knew if I carried on smoking I was heading the same way. It was bad enough that both my sons were deprived of a father, but I wasn't going to deprive them of a mother. Not yet, if I could help it. And I didn't . My children all grew up healthy and only one (my little baby) smokes now.

So here's my method.

You need to have a run up to giving up. A period of grace while you are still allowed to smoke. You might decide to switch to vaping or patches during this time but for me the hard way (cold turkey) was actually the easiest way in the end.

The really important reason for this period of grace is to give yourself time to imagine a life without smoking. To prepare for it. To imagine the pitfalls and prepare strategies. Those who try to give up instantly are surprised by the pitfalls and those who use patches and the like aren't really giving up at all. The space to think about it gives you time to remember what you love about smoking and what you hate. To find replacements for those things that you love and to build up a real disgust for those things you hate. You can smoke as much as you like during this time, and I did, but you must think about each cigarette and why you like / loathe it. Record which cigarettes are most important to you. For me it was the first one in the morning. The first one after the 'fast'.

At no point did I allow the idea that I was giving up 'my best friend' or my 'prop'. Whenever that thought occurred to me I kept telling myself that the evil nicotine was out to rule and order my life … and I never did like authority! This I think for me was the crux. Identifying the cigarette not as a friend but as something which was trying to control my life and removing other options from me because of its very high cost. You can think of it if you like as an unfair tax which you refuse to pay which in fact it actually is!

So the big idea was to buy myself a really pretty diary in which to record my promises to myself not to smoke. On a daily basis I had to make a promise to myself that for just that day … I would not smoke. It had to be a nice diary that I liked as an extra incentive not to waste it. I don't remember where I got this idea but although it seems simple. It turned out to be brilliant.

All I had to do each day, from day one, was to take up my pretty pen and my sweet scented flower diary and record the words "Today I will not smoke". Now the reason this helped me, is that I'm both honest and stubborn. Both to a fault. So when I make a promise, I either fulfil it or suffer greatly from guilt and have to make amends several times over. Since I didn't have any idea what form making amends would take, in this case, failure to stick to my own promise to myself was not an option. But that was OK, each promise only lasted 24 hours and I was free to make a different decision the next day. Except as I said before I was not allowed the first cigarette. So, every day I dutifully recorded the promise after reminding myself that I wasn't allowed the first cigarette. Then I was stuck in my own promise for the whole day.

There were other little assists and props which I used, some of which seem a bit ridiculous now but are made less ridiculous by the fact that they worked. One was to buy a pack of "bickiepegs". I'm not sure these even exist now, but they are, or were ultra hardened biscuits which threaded onto a ribbon, to be given to teething babies. They weren't sweet or particularly pleasant. They were marginally more satisfying than ballpoint pens for chewing and sucking.

Nutritionally I supported myself with orange juice and vitamin and mineral supplements including zinc and the full spectrum of the B vitamins.

Yes of course I got into a Maltesers habit and put on weight. I also got into a small 'Bourbon whisky' habit. This last habit was partly down to the fact I realised one thing I loved about cigarettes was that smoky 'burn' on the back of the mouth and the throat. It was a good replacement for that but, for a while I 'used it' a bit more than I should because it filled the boredom gaps. I wasn't particularly satisfied with my life at the time, and I had a partner who didn't live with me but disappeared off to his own flat each evening. This could have been more dangerous than it was in the end, but I was partly held back by the fact that I didn't have enough money to afford a big habit. Also, my stomach wouldn't take strong alcohol for long. I wasn't going to give up cigarettes only to die of pancreatic cancer like someone I knew who liked a nip or ten of whisky. *But* I did have to deal with the weight gain further down the line. Don't let that stop you, though. That's one of the addicts regular excuses. Just be aware of all those and don't let them creep in. Oh and see the piggy bank section later in the book. Putting the money that you would have spent on the cigarettes into your piggy bank is another way of getting a sense of that self-rewarding you might feel you're missing. Don't forget to pat yourself on the back too or treat yourself to a wonderful long bath followed by dressing in something glorious that doesn't smell!

Anyway. I don't know at what stage I realised I had finally conquered the evil weed. But I do know I still had cravings for years and just the occasional one even now. But giving up a drug is like grief. You think about it all day for three days. Every day for three weeks. Every week for three months. And you never forget for the whole of your life. Even now I 'fancy a fag' from time to time and will happily sit next to a smoker and inhale their second hand smoke. For years I dreamed of smoking and woke up feeling guilty. Now I miss those dreams a little! What I will never do is put the first lit cigarette in my mouth. The first … The only one I can't have.

Overeating

So then I had to give up eating. This was another one that I had to do more than once and in fact I did spend most of my adult life overweight but I only dieted twice. Both times on a low-carb diet and both were successful. The first time I kept the weight off for around 4 years but then it crept back on and I was back to where I started and stayed overweight for a long time. I only succeeded the second time because it was a life or possible death decision just like it had been with the smoking. My methods were similar to the first time but this time I had a very short time to lose quite a lot of weight, but it was also very important that I didn't weaken my body in any way. In fact I had to strengthen it for a big operation. In order to do it successfully I needed to feel I was making a very real contribution to my chances of living. I had to positively enjoy the experience and feel I wasn't depriving myself but actually giving myself something else. See frugal dieting.

Over buying and over spending

This is my latest battle, but possibly the easiest since there are no physical cravings only psychological ones and my northern 'bloody mindedness' is stronger than my softy self-rewarder.

FASHION

Here is the absolute joy of frugalism. You really don't have to be unfashionable, badly dressed or badly clothed to be frugal. I'm going to start back to front here and address hair and make-up first just to get it out of the way.

Hair. All my life I was as frugal as it's possible to be about hair-dressing, well I just had long hair! It never needed cutting, blow drying straightening or curling. Unfortunately, as a little old lady, I now have short hair as the result of cutting it deliberately to avoid chemo fallout. The fall out never materialised but it was too late. I now have short hair. It costs a bit more because to stay short and attractive it does need a little cutting from time to time. Around once every 3 months it costs me 25 euros … Ouch. But until I can get a friend to understand the whacky shape that I want, I just have to grit my teeth and pay the artist for his work. Of course you can get a friend to cut your hair. I'm afraid my closest hairdressing friend knows just the one old-lady style and I'm not prepared to compromise on that. I also decided to stop using hair colour on all of my hair and just use it on my naturally grey streaks. I was never going to be very normal, so I colour that part blue or purple or however I feel (I usually default to blue). I use only around 2 pots of colour a year for such a small part of my hair. So it costs me under a tenner a year. Interestingly my young and very lovely daughter also chooses to colour just small parts of her hair which she bleaches first. I imagine she might spend all of 15 pounds a year in total on colour. She will, I'm sure, have similar or maybe slightly lower hair cutting costs. So we're talking around 100 pounds or euros a year. A significant outlay but for some of us hair is very important.

Make up. Just don't bother having more than one of each make up item. You don't need more. Replace only when absolutely needed. Or give up makeup altogether. Don't buy other cosmetic items. Make them yourself or gratefully accept them for Xmas & birthdays!

Frugal warriors might want to give up make up altogether. Let your laugh lines show! Make your lips look more beautiful by genuinely smiling, and let your eyes twinkle with good humour.

Clothes. Now on to the important question of frugal clothing buying. Having been a bit too spendy on clothes in the past, now I'm born-again frugal. I have to admit I learned a lot from a wealthier friend here. When I was very poorly and living on very very little my friend took to sending me little gifts to cheer me up. This friend is naturally frugal too but can afford quality when she wants to. She has a love for Merino wool and over a year sent me two cardigans and a jumper in Merino wool. When they were in the sale … well, she's not daft! These were still expensive items which I would never have considered buying but I knew Merino's reputation for being durable and smell-free. And I had always coveted such items. These items have become absolute favourites for me. When I had to find something for my son's wedding and I wanted a bolero top I went for a Merino wool one. I knew absolutely that it would become a new 'posh' favourite that would be worn again and again. Since the dress was second-hand at 15 euros and the shoes just 6.99 I didn't feel the total was too much to spend, for a beloved son's wedding. I actually felt more attractive that night than I have done … well forever actually. Shame nobody took a photograph, so I can't prove it. Well, who takes pictures of little old ladies even if they are just drunk enough to imagine themselves as stunning as Cinderella? I do have to admit that was just the dress for the evening. In fact I spent a little more on a dress for the day. But once again I'd found a beautiful dress at half-price and in this case I spent the money because it was something I knew I would wear over and over again as day wear. This is important as I don't go to parties or functions very often. In fact I'm something of a hermit. Back to the subject of Merino wool. I have since bought socks for travel in this material because I travel light. Merino wool can be worn much longer. I'll happily wear these socks for 3 days instead of one. So I can honestly say expensive clothes can make for cheaper travel and less washing. Less washing and less plastic shedding particles are also better for the environment. Yes, I know we don't all have a generous friend. My advice is to keep your eyes peeled for labels in charity shops in more well-to-do areas. You might get lucky! And Maybe instead of blowing 60 quid on six items in Primark, just keep your eyes open on the internet for the end of season sales on really good quality clothing. Fewer, better clothes = more happiness because your clothes are actually nicer. Not as much cupboard / drawer space will be filled with rubbish which you'll never wear. Environmentally its much better as well as being less fuel for the sweat shop trade. You may cry that you are giving them work that they need, but this isn't the whole story. Sweat shop tyranny supports only the greedy and not the needy. People buying less but higher-quality clothing will support the poorer in society more overall.

So, make yourself a list of what you really like to wear and how little you can get away with and bit by bit replace the rubbish by quality. If you're feeling a bit spendy and can afford it, buy one nice piece of clothing that will give you joy for years.

I'm not going to bang on about making do and mending because if you love your clothes more, you'll look after them and want them to last longer anyway. Frugal warriors will already happily be living on a set of clothing and a spare set or two at most and will be less encumbered for it. I don't need to tell them to search out charity shops and gratefully receive cast-offs! In fact a Frugal warrior will tend to gravitate towards better quality clothing rather than paying a cent for something that won't last.

CARS AND DRIVING

This is a short section because I'm by no means an expert in car buying, having only ever owned two cars in my life and the first one was a dog lasting less than a year before passing it on free to a friend. One thing I can say is that where I live it's definitely cheaper to buy new than second hand. In Spain the second hand car market is over-buoyant.

Car ownership is not frugal depending on where you live. If you live in a city, it's almost certainly not frugal. But it may be absolutely necessary for your lifestyle or for getting to work. But always factor in transport costs when deciding where to work and where to live! My daughter was able to give up car ownership partly because she didn't enjoy it anyway but partly by simply not going for jobs that weren't on direct and reliable transport links. Giving up the car has enabled her to focus on house buying instead of renting which definitely looks like a win to me.

If you have to have a car then my opinion, for what it's worth, is that it's worth buying a car new or semi new and keeping it until it's absolutely died. One reason for this is that you get to understand your own car. You know which bits have been replaced and which need replacing. You're in charge of the when and where, when it comes to preventative maintenance. The first years are costly. However if you keep it a long time and its properly maintained those costs do go down if you bought well in the first place. Our old Fiesta was bought second hand at 4 years old. It was relatively younger in mileage. It's now nearly 20 years old. The maintenance costs have been very low, and I would say we've paid an average of less than 200 pounds per year in maintenance in the last 10 years and that includes new tyres. Perhaps we got lucky? I'd like to think I chose well. A good car with an excellent engine which had hardly been used. From a dealer who had taken it in part exchange for another job 'perk' car.

We always diagnose our own car faults these days after one garage quoted us 300 euros to change 3 brake drums. The problem with the brakes turned out to be a broken 'bleed nipple'. Cost of diagnosis and repair 30 euros.

Another fault we had recently the part was going to cost 75 euros so we found one online for 15 and took it to our local mechanic.

If you have frugal friends why not discuss sharing a car and of course the insurance which should be lower than the sum of its two or more holders. Also if you must have a new car its worth looking at whether it's more expensive to buy new, lease or buy second hand and factor in maintenance costs etc.

Watch out for car hire schemes and scams

When hiring cars abroad if you have kids, make sure you take any necessary baby or booster seats. Or if you have friends and family who live there ask them to get hold of second hand for you. The cost of one set of second hand seats can be less than the price of the cost of hire for a week! If you visit the same place regularly this can save you a fortune in hire costs and a load of luggage space and hassle. Last year consumers in the UK spent £475 million on unforeseen car hire costs.

Watch out for and avoid expensive insurance traps.

Read the terms and conditions. Car rental companies must show hidden charges upfront.

When you pick up the vehicle, inspect it and note any damage, take pictures or video on your phone. And note them on your form. No damage is too small to note down. Companies have been found to charge more than once for the same damage.

If you've signed up for an extra damage insurance which you don't need and which doesn't apply to some regularly damaged bits of the car anyway, you need a huge limit on your credit card to cover the deposit. This can be up to 2,000. Most people don't realise that you have to pay upfront and then reclaim any money paid. I won't go into all the possible ways car hire companies can squeeze you because its all covered on the internet. Make yourself aware!

Driving lessons

If you are young and can afford it, take your lessons and pass your test as soon as you can whether or not you can afford a car. You will find it easier to pass than an older person, and then that test pass is in the bag (using the money for driving might also save you from sandpapering the inside of your head so badly every Friday night). You will also be treated as a more experienced driver for insurance purposes when you finally get around to buying a car. And having top up lessons at that time will pay for themselves in premium reduction. Also, you will be able to look at car share schemes and leasing at any time. You may also get access to better jobs merely by having that license and you don't even have to own a car!

Save money on lessons by having a couple of hours of practice with an eligible adult for every hour of paid lessons. If you can't get on that person's insurance go practise on private land just to give you a bit more confidence in your manoeuvring. All that slow speed stuff and remembering to look in the mirrors is what costs more failed tests than anything else. And here I have experience. Your driving instructor can take you out on the fast roads and help you correct any bad habits.

Driving lessons are the sort of present your parents and other relatives are often happy to pay for. They will see it as an investment in your future and will be happy you're spending some of your money and time on this kind of 'sensible' plan.

Maintenance of tyres

If you drive on lots of steep roads swap your tyres from side to side each year if you can, to avoid uneven wear. We don't because we aren't mechanically minded and a trip to the garage to do it would cost more than the value in tyres saved. We do have to change our tyres more often because of it, though.

HOUSING

Wow, this is a tricky one! Because housing costs, certainly in the UK, are through the roof these days. So it depends on what you have, what you want and what you need. Many of us who need to be frugal don't have parents who can help us get a deposit on a house together. I'm just going to provide you with a few 'creative' ideas for you to think about if you are stuck in a housing situation you don't like. It's very difficult to find truly frugal housing solutions but being frugal can certainly help you pay your mortgage off sooner or save for deposits or improvements.

First my take on why we are in this situation especially in the UK and even more so in the big popular cities. Most people don't really understand how politics impacts their daily lives. Did you know for example that voting for parties who advocate tax cuts for the rich, results in those rich spending more money on property? This in turn results in higher property prices. Then everyone (except the rich) have to work longer to pay mortgages and rent. Making the rich richer can only make the poor poorer.

When I was young, there seemed to be a reasonable balance in the price of housing. We had a sort of unwritten 1/3rds rule. Your housing costs were 1/3rd of your (single) income. Your utilities another 1/3rd and the last 1/3rd for everything else. Now housing costs are so high most people can't make the maths work. There are a few 'shuffles' you can employ if you already have something. But getting on that first rung seems almost impossible for young families. The only answer seeming to be to put off, or even decide not to have children at all. Here are the shuffle ideas which I have personal experience of, followed by a few thoughts on how you might be able to get your first place.

At the end of this subject I have put a few ideas for if your housing status is very unstable. Meanwhile here are some buying ideas.

My son and his wife were stuck in a house that had belonged to him in a previous relationship. Although it was a nice enough house they really wanted somewhere which was theirs. Somewhere nearer to their work. They were stuck in negative equity at the time, so I suggested that they rent out to his brother who needed a home at the time. This suited both parties. It gave one son a way out of his situation and a trustworthy tenant. The other got cheaper accommodation for a couple of years until he himself was ready to move on and buy his own house. Of course this isn't without its complexities. Under certain buy to let mortgages you aren't supposed to rent to a relative and effectively the mortgage was backed partly by the letting income from the first house. A little complicated. Since my son's brother was his half brother and had a different surname, it worked out for them. I did warn one son the other was bound to leave his house in what he'd consider a bit of a mess. I was unsurprised and unsympathetic when there was a little dispute about that. Neither party could deny the arrangement had suited their purpose getting the first son a little way out of his negative equity situation and the second a little way into his saving up for a deposit if that's what he chose to do with the saving. Needless to say the slight dispute about the scruffy carpet etc. was very quickly put in the past. Renting to another person you know and trust is a reasonable way to make a side step in your housing situation or a step up when you can't sell your current house or at least not for the money you want. You do need to make it a win-win and be prepared for small amounts of wear and tear.

Buy a dump!

This can work if you have cash or your own home of any equity value and access to credit. But you have to have courage and some DIY skills as well as the ability to live in less than perfect conditions for a while.

We wanted to upgrade from a low value home to a better low value home. We didn't want to go through the danger of selling the one before buying the other. We'd identified the street we wanted to live on and knew the price we would have to pay for a large house in very bad condition. That happened to be a similar amount of money to the amount we could easily get at that time (pre market-crash) as a home improvement loan. It's worth remembering that at that time it was way too easy to get loans and that this may not work now. We simply got a home improvement loan for the first house, spent it on buying the second house for cash and paid back the loan by the sale of the first house. Slightly on the edge, but not illegal. After all we were improving the value of our home. Just not the first home. This only works on very low value property and if you own it outright or nearly, so its not available to everyone. It works only because a dump is so far from mortgageable that an owner will take a very low offer for cash. You also have to know at least something about renovating or be prepared to live in a dump for some time but since this book is about frugal living its safe to imagine that most readers would be prepared to live in less than ideal circumstances for an overall improvement in their long-term situation. We have also flipped another dump since then. The house we live in now was also originally a dump. Unfortunately, I can't claim we were as financially successful with this one, but we were hit by a currency crisis. However, it's amazing what you can live with when you are forced to do so. If you have a small amount of money lots of courage and no other hope of improving your living situation renovating a dump may be the way to go.

House sharing

Buy a mortgage together with a friend or a group of friends. Make sure you get all the legal paperwork sorted out really well. At some time in the future your plans are going to change, and one of you may want to sell before the other. Make sure you discuss this and have plans in place beforehand. You could decide on a plan that lets one of you walk away and hand the keys back without needing to continue paying the mortgage or getting any share … if necessary. Otherwise, the prospect of one person suddenly not paying their share could put you right back in crisis.

Renting part of your home

Renting out part of your home is not illegal, but it may not be comfortable. However, if the alternative is losing your home altogether, you may find its a better option at least temporarily.

Housing crisis?

If you already have a home but it's looking like you may lose it due to mounting debts you can consider downsizing so as not to lose the prospect of ever owning anything again. But before you consider selling, look at the debt management groups who can help you get out of your financial situation. I have experience only of Payplan and they literally saved us from the agony of homelessness and destitution. We are still paying off our substantial debts at an affordable rate per month. Not easy, but better than the alternative.

Other living ideas

If you are renting or have to leave home for any reason and it looks like you might lose your place, look at **couchsurfing.com** The people who are members of couchsurfing are committed to sharing their space with people who want or need some temporary accommodation. It's usually limited to a few days at a time and isn't anything like a permanent solution but you can take time out from crashing on parents and friends sofas and get to know some new and interesting people.

Housesitting

www.trustedhousesitters.com

This isn't a permanent solution but can be a good way of travelling round the country, meeting new people and if you can work from a laptop it could be an idea especially if you have some kind of base but don't want to stay there permanently, for example if you are currently living with parents or friends or an ex-partner.

Housesitting can be paired with living in a static caravan or motor-home during the summer months.

Living caravans, trailers and tiny homes

If you have the courage to take on a project, read Tiny Houses Built With Recycled Materials. Or look at a posher version

www.tinyhouseuk.co.uk

There is some question over whether the government wants to make tiny homes illegal in the UK. Surely they would help to solve a housing crisis.

Communes and cooperatives

Start at

diggersanddreamers.org.uk

You have to be flexible and commit yourself to making an effort but you can try it on for size. It might just be your way of living. I think in another life, if I didn't have children young I might have tried it.

Squatting

Technically illegal there are loopholes

www.gov.uk/squatting-law

Read the lovely book by Catrina Davis - Homesick: Why I live in a shed. Not a cheap book I'm afraid but then even homeless authors need to eat!

Being Nomadic (Homeless)

Not recommended of course. But read: The Salt Path By Raynor Winn. There's a romance to reading the story but being homeless is a horrible existence and to be avoided at all costs. If you are facing homelessness, get help and advice now before it happens.

england.shelter.org.uk

FRUGAL DIY SKILLS

Maybe it goes without saying that if you do it yourself you can save a great deal of money. With building of course you have to be strong and fit enough to do it. I've now reached an age where I know I have to hand over more of the work on my house to younger people. Sometimes to professionals but sometimes to lovely neighbours. Just yesterday a neighbour came over and climbed on my roof and sealed my roof light. A job I undoubtedly would have had to pay two hundred euros to a professional for or a hundred to a bodger. My lovely neighbour wouldn't accept a penny!

One thing I've found is that doing it yourself goes through several phases. There is "it needs doing and I can't afford it". Quickly followed by "I can't possibly do it I wouldn't have a clue how", followed by an extended period of procrastination. Followed by the problem getting bigger and more insoluble, followed by finding out how to do it and having a go. Making a better job of it than you thought usually comes next. Finally the pleasure of success and going on to do the other eight similar jobs you thought were beyond you. I'm not going to tell stories about all my DIY adventures here but purely because I've had to I've done rather a lot. I've replaced Victorian sash windows, fixed guttering, pointed walls. I've fitted fireplaces and stoves, built walls, hung doors including their frames, built gates, plumbed in toilets and built more internal walls and fitted furniture. I've tiled more walls and floors and laid more underfloor heating than I care to remember. Each time I've had to pull the builder out of myself kicking and screaming as I can't say I love it until I stand back and survey a job well (or sometimes just well-enough) done.

I have one simple rule for this kind of job to make sure that you don't muck it up or leave it half done. Make a plan and especially a list of all the materials and tools you will need. Unsuccessful bodgers are those who get started, don't have all the tools or materials needed and underestimate the time it takes to do a job.

So here are my Frugal DIY hints

1 Get a notebook and pencil.

2 Find a Youtube vid on how to do what you want to do. Get a coffee and watch it … Take notes.

3 Check your notes twice by watching other people doing it a different way. Or check it in a comprehensive DIY guide like Collins complete DIY manual.

4 Take time about buying, begging and borrowing tools. If you require major tools try to borrow first. Failing that get second hand or hire from a tool shop.

5 Check your own toolkit for all the smaller hand tools.

So have a go. A can-do mindset can be developed over time. You may find your first adventures into Frugal DIY are scary. The more successes you have the more fearless you'll become and the quicker it will happen next time. You don't have to start out with a love of DIY to become an expert and to end up being proud of your achievements. At one time my husband professed a fear of drills and ladders and I pooh-poohed him for it but his disquiet was real … to him. However, he became our electrician, under the supervision of a qualified electrician of course. Along the way he was forced to do some repetitive drilling and plugging to attach a conduit to hollow brick walls. He became an absolute expert in this having made all the annoying mistakes it was possible to make in the first couple of days, finding out what really worked by trial and error. The truth is that experts in any field are very often those who have made all the mistakes. You can learn from them now because of Youtube, especially if you can't bear reading tedious how-to instruction books.

CHEAP FURNISHING AND BUILDING MATERIALS

Sofas and beds chairs, etc.

Am I just lucky? I'm not sure. I always seem to get just what I want or something else that I wanted from the IKEA seconds shop. I would say we almost never pay full price for any piece of furniture. By being patient and being prepared to wait until the bargains came up I've been able to get a pair of beds and a pair of mattresses (mattresses first as you can sleep on those!) in two separate trips. This gave me far too much pleasure because my friend who took me on the second trip in his van was certain I'd be disappointed when I said, somewhat cockily, that I almost always got what I wanted by sheer good luck. And luck was indeed with me that day. My friend was what I can only describe as 'gobsmacked'. There is no second hand furniture market here so we've always had to buy new. In the UK however, I was pretty good at second hand furniture shopping and bought some very interesting and unusual furniture for 'a song' over my single parent years. Auctions can also be a really good source of old furniture you can upcycle and even sell on! Look for cheap unconsidered items with broken handles or chips, etc. but which are made of good solid wood and which are simple and functional in design and you can't go far wrong. Avoid furniture which has very ornate design or which can't be used in more than one way. Know what you can afford to pay and keep that level low unless your love for it is intense!

Here in Spain we go Ikea shopping when we have extra money and a desire to improve the house. We always carry a saw and hammer and screwdriver set in the car for the bargains that we have to dismantle to get into our little Fiesta. It's just amazing how much you can get in there. I was gutted to have said a polite no to an Ikea employee. He'd offered me as many more as I wanted of a certain type of weatherproof chair that they were selling at 7 euros each. I could only get 6 into my car. I would have liked more for my classroom. I changed my mind later, realising they were cheap enough to pay for transport, but unfortunately that employee was on his lunch break. The others weren't prepared to bring more of the chairs out for me. Oh well you win some you lose some.

Storage

One of the items its easiest to save money on is storage.

As far as acquiring wood for DIY projects, one of the cheapest sources we've found is floor boarding. I don't know if it was cheap here (in Spain) because it was an unpopular material. We did find it to be the cheapest source of cheap shelving for my workshop. Shelving on the bracket system is versatile and much cheaper than any other form of temporary furnishing. Of course if you rent, you will have to ask your landlord's permission to put up shelf brackets. But once again you can get more shelves for fewer holes in the wall with these systems.

I've bought cupboards for my living room in IKEA's 'op shop' My space for cupboards was built on either side of my wood burner. One of the easiest ways to build in furniture and benching is to use what we call 'razzas'. Their proper name is 'rasillones'. These are a very long large, extremely lightweight, roof bricks. They are more usually used to slot between lintels when building roofs. I used them to build insulated partition walls, and within those I put cupboards which were actually wardrobe units with some cut down wardrobe doors. One wardrobe door made two of the lower doors. I avoided the need to finish the cut edges by putting them both cut edge down and therefore totally invisible. Because IKEA units are built on very few simple modular designs it's easy to buy the parts as they come up.

Built in furniture

In Spain, wood for carpentry and construction can be rather expensive. We've opted for very popular and traditional built in 'slab built' storage. Basically this is just sides and tops constructed in building materials. We use rasillones, and finished in tiles or painted cement render. Cement is then trowelled or poured over to provide the strength, without which they can be rather fragile. They are really quick to use and very inexpensive as side supports too and can be built very rapidly using mortar or yeso (quick drying plaster).

We have built many internal wall and cupboard units, also using 'razzas' as the cross pieces including bathroom benching and workshop benching'. I've also built partition walls around my fireplace using 2 layers of 'razzas'. My favourite project was the shelves for my pantry. I then shuttered them with wood and poured a thick layer (about 10cm) of concrete on top to make them very cooling. I may ask my local marble supplier for his offcuts which he used to dump in the 'campo'. I know he has to pay for them to be removed and therefore may be happy to offload his waste on me. These could make a nice cool cleanable surface as long as I don't mind spending some time doing a bit of a jigsaw and then grouting the cracks. On the other hand large wall or floor tiles (when on offer) are a very easy clean surface. I often buy the plainest of these and have used them for movable work surfaces for my job as well as surfaces on built in workshop and bathroom storage. My outside wood store was also built by the rasillones and cement pour method. I'm not sure if these are available in England. In fact I'm pretty sure they aren't. However get yourself some building supply info because something similar will probably be available. And If you can't find them you can always use thin bricks. If in the end you don't like the open shelf look you can always partially or wholly cover with cupboard doors at a later date.

Recycling

One thing all of us need to overcome is our inner embarrassment at recycling things left on the street. We seem naturally to shy away from being seen by our neighbours out in the street taking what could be seen by some as 'rubbish'. But this is a valueless response. After all, if it was stacked up in a yard for sale we'd have no problem with it.

In our village a local construction that was never finished during the housing crash here, has just thrown out all the left over plasterboard. Some quite big pieces. We happen to have a few projects that need plasterboard. My inner frugalist overcame my husband's natural anxiety and we asked the local shopkeeper if it was chucked or waiting. He told us the people clearing the site had put it in the bin and the binmen took it out again. So it was ours for the taking. This is not the first time I've overcome my own embarrassment to take home a treasure. When we bought our first house together I saw a Victorian fireplace in a skip. It was left overnight and clearly rubbish and it came home with me and was put to very good use replacing a horrible 1950s surround in my Victorian house. The key if you aren't sure is to ask the owner of the home in question if you can take the item. Or ask the nearest neighbour when the item was thrown out. If it's clearly been or going to be over night and its clearly waste (for example by the bins) then I think morally you're right to recycle. Be prepared to give it back if asked. If there is any doubt though, leave it where you see it. But don't fight shy of recycling from embarrassment only.

LIVING FRUGALLY, GADGETS AND WHITE GOODS

We are naturally spendthrift. Especially when it comes to technology and gadgets. But to be fair the gadgets we buy are those that help us to save money. One of my favourite is a vacuum sealer machine. These are quite expensive, so it took me many months to decide to buy one even though I'd been itching to do it. Now I'm really glad I did. The greatest expense is the bags. They work by sucking the air out of the bag and then sealing it. This keeps your food fresher and less prone to freezer burn. It also helps you to pack more into a small freezer and to identify your foods better. Another advantage is that you can cook your foods in the bag. The biggest cost to be factored in is the cost of the bags which come in at anything from 8 cents to 35 cents a bag depending on the size. You can also buy the bags on rolls. I bought a medium sized bag first at 12 cents a bag but then decided I wanted more options for sizes of bags. I started by cutting down my medium size bags into half-sizes by sealing the other end and cutting down the middle. Then I decided to go back and buy some more that gave me more options so I picked up a roll. Then my husband pointed out that the most expensive size actually gave you a lot more of the plastic material, weight for weight than any of the other sizes and that if we were going to be cutting down for smaller items anyway it was the most economical way to buy. You can occasionally get a good deal at Aldi or Lidl in the UK.

DIY gadgets we've bought

Well pump - this is a necessity because we live off grid as far as the water supply

UPS (uninterruptable power supply) this is important because of the power outages which are very common where we are. As we go to off grid electricity they will be even more important on every computer device.

Power hoist - we bought this, used it and sold it for almost as much as we paid for it.

Board lifter for plasterboard

Timer plugs because I'm terrible for forgetting to turn off heaters. So when I have a short period of time in a room which needs to be heated I have a 50 minute timer plug which we bought in England. This turns off my heater and saves me getting an ear bashing from my husband.

Here is a hack from a friend of mine who has been stocking her own house and two gites with white goods. *"Especially in or near a well-heeled area, the thing is to look out for [is] MIELE or similar quality appliances second hand. People put in new kitchens and laundries and chuck out perfectly good free standing appliances or give them to the builder to get rid of [who then] sell them on eBay. I got what was then a current model MIELE washing machine for £65 from a couple who were doing just that.*

As it's expensive to transport large items like this, they are only bought by locals. So if on the day the Miele washing machine is being sold, three people want one, the price will be bid up. But on another day you are the only person who wants a machine, and you pick it up for much less.

Second hand good quality is better as it's less likely to go wrong. Certain parts of a machine such as the pump is basically a consumable item and will eventually fail. You can get replacements from eSpares and similar website - it's cheaper going direct to their site than going via eBay".

Look after your equipment and clean your pump sump out regularly.

Keep your eyes out for upgrade/ refurb bargains. Techy gear and crafty gear are often upgraded when a newer machine with more features comes out. This sort of stuff often bores people when they buy it on a whim and then realise they can't or won't use it for some reason. We've bought plotter cutters for our business for a quarter of the price when people want to upgrade. We now never buy a brand-new computer. Of course the latter does generally require some hardware knowledge to choose.

I did get a brand new laptop for Xmas because you can't simply replace dodgy parts so that was, for me, important to get new. I got a none Windows one because they are cheaper and need less maintenance.

MY STRANGE ADDICTION TO THE OLD FASHIONED BUTTER KNIFE

I'm weirdly attracted to butter knives in second hand shops, car boot sales, vide-greniers and on ebay. I can't walk past a bundle of butter knives without sizing them up for utility in my kitchen, my workshop and my tool box. A more universal tool has yet to be invented and yet, although one really good one will do, I have dozens. I buy them on my travels all over Europe. I make the fact that I teach crafts my excuse every time I feel the need to 'invest' some of my euros in yet another set. I have large utilitarian ones with chunky faux bone handles from a British charity shop. Ones where the faux bone handle is half broken off that I intend to make new handles for. Dainty bakelite ones from the turn of the last century, which I bought from a cutlery specialist called Jennifer on Ebay. Big flat silver plated ones from a Barcelona antique shop. A beautiful set of green handled Swedish ones which I got my friend to negotiate for, bought and then dropped one of into the drain in the big barn which was an antiques emporium. That missing knife still tugs at my heart strings and my conscience! I even have a half set of real steel ones with bone handles which go rusty if I don't take care of them and which, I remember, came from a Covent Garden flea market stall, and which I beat the vendor down to six quid for by telling him they were going in my toolkit. And they did, even though I suspect they may be very old indeed. I am not a sentimental collector at all. Things have to have a use for me to treasure them and anything that has more than one use, like the butter knife pulled me with an irresistible force.

I wonder if it goes back to the time a maiden great aunt who was a bit of a hoarder of tasteful homewares invited me, from her deathbed, to take my pick of her boxed cutlery. A young teenager at the time I selected a box of pretty pretty silver teaspoons. I can't say that I was particularly connected to the aunt and so my selection was based purely on aesthetics. I wasn't connected to the spoons either and only kept them a handful of years until I cashed them in for some money to invest in an antique clothes business. I wonder if I'd chosen butter knives whether I'd have kept them and used them and remembered the aunt better by them. The truth is, it's more likely I'd have bent them out of shape using them as:

Screwdrivers, paint mixers, polymer clay cutters, stencil appliers, carving tools, paint spatulas, pry bars, bottle top openers, door wedges, watch case openers, pointing tools for mortar and grouting and cleaning tools for tiling.

Just occasionally however, one might be discovered in my kitchen drawer or in the sink with a smear of butter on it!

HOME HEATING AND COOLING HACKS

The UK and parts of the US don't have a problem with too much heat and some don't have a problem with too much cold. Nevertheless some poorer Spanish rural societies have hacks which are well worth looking at from a frugal point of view, wherever you live.

Solar gain and solar loss

You want to add the least possible heating or cooling to your home as this saves money (and energy). Plus air conditioning is unhealthy and so are many forms of heating.

It sounds negligible but let the sun in, in winter, whenever it's shining. Also air your house at least once a week (once a day is better) when it's dry. Houses where you never open a window get damp and unhealthy. You can get a build up of black mould, which is really dangerous to your health. Many people blame their landlords for mouldy houses. To be fair sometimes they do need to do remedial work, however often the problem is more to do with under-airing. We are all so busy trying to keep cold out that we forget that stale damp air is very detrimental to the house and its occupants.

When it gets dark closing blinds, curtains etc. keeps you warmer.

The Spanish under the table heater

Here in Spain most living rooms are set up a little differently from in England, in winter at least.

A table of medium or dining table height is set between sofas and armchairs and covered with a thick cloth down to the ground. Over this is a glass surface. Under the table they put a heater which used to be a brazier in the old days. Now its more commonly a small round electric or gas heater. The thinking behind this is very simple and delightfully frugal. To keep warm while sitting still watching TV eating or just chatting with friends you simply pull the cloth over your knees. If the weather is very cold, you can pull it up to your shoulders. The rest of the house is often completely unheated because when you're moving around you feel the cold less. I find it works extremely well if you just have background heat to keep the chill off other rooms. A 400-watt heater is enough to keep a room you barely use or you use only when being active from feeling too chilly

How to make a very low cost heater or under table burner

Very low heat burner to keep the chill off a room AKA a flower pot heater. Yes, some people want to debunk it by measuring simply the BTUs (British Thermal Units) but what they don't realise is that a candle simply burning on a table top will just go straight up to the ceiling whereas one under a plant pot (with this plant pot additionally under the table) will heat the pot letting the heat out in a more 'radiant' way. The candle doesn't burn quite as fast either because it's got slightly less oxygen so it lasts longer. So yes, you may only get exactly the same BTUs with and without the plant pot. However, this method may be more effective in keeping the chill off a room for a longer period, and just a little safer too. Simply place a candle or oil burner (I have a little olive oil burning lamp - refined olive oil can be pretty cheap here) in a large plant pot base and use a couple of strips of ceramic tile or a couple of small thermal bricks to separate the base from the top. Just pop the un-drilled plant pot upside down over the top. If your plant pot already has a hole in you can close it with a nut and bolt and a large washer. There are some more complex designs using a double pot on the internet, but I find this simple version works well. Make sure you put it somewhere it can't get knocked over. This is pretty easy on a tiled Spanish kitchen floor which is where I have mine. These heaters are also very useful in greenhouses to keep frost at bay.

Major heating expenses, wood burning or pellet stoves?

You can get an insert for your wood burning stove to put pellets in if you run out of wood. You have to keep feeding it, but it can save you from a firewood shortage.

Pellet stoves can't be backwards converted, but a pellet stove with a feed can be very economical. The cost of these has come down quite a lot, so you can get one for around 500 pounds but you will need to get someone to install it for you. I would say in a room used infrequently a pellet stove is a great option because it warms quickly when turned on and turns off equally quickly.

Wood burning stove hacks

Dry lemon and orange peels on your stove, or next to it if the surface is very hot. It makes your room smell amazing and the peels make excellent fire lighters.

A metal and glass plunger coffee maker is great used on a wood-burning stove. Boil the water and put on the coffee first then just leave it on the stove. It keeps hot and the flavour intensifies until you are ready to use it. I think it can be comparable with the taste of coffee machine expresso.

I have recently seen a stove top kettle design that wraps round the stove pipe. This was for a small rocket stove and I haven't yet seen one for my stove pipe size. But what a fab idea! I'll be keeping my eyes open for one of these or even asking someone to make me one.

Keep cool!

In Spain we have exterior sun blinds or shutters to keep out fierce summer sun. If you are buying sun blinds, there are several grades. The more expensive ones are better insulated.

If you have tiled floors, mopping floors can cool the whole house by a process of evaporation as long as you have a good airflow and a low enough humidity. Wiping down other surfaces can help too. This is Spanish grandma wisdom and it really works. Grandma maybe doesn't know she's a scientist!

Put a sun canopy in front of your back door if its in a sunny position. Ours faces west and has the sun all day from around 11 am in summer. The canopy keeps the worst of the heat off the back of our house. A white or light coloured one reflects heat. Heat avoided is cooling not needed. With these simple tricks we find that even though our summer temperatures regularly reach 37 degrees and can get to 40 degrees centigrade outside we still don't need air conditioning.

FRUGAL CLEANING

One of my friends, who is normally pretty frugal told me when we were discussing frugal household products that 'green' products were more expensive! I was excited that she said that because I was happy to have a myth to disprove. They are not more expensive to make but the up-sold smartly packaged ones are expensive to buy!

Nowhere is it more obvious that you don't need so many products. Not having so many toxic products going down your drains is green, and it is frugal. But it really doesn't have to be either / or. If you find a milder washing powder causes a build up in your machine or on your clothes you can switch back to a stronger (more toxic) cleaner for a week. If your drains clog up because you aren't using very strong degreasers, even if you do pour hot water down them once in a while then if have to put a drain cleaner down the sink every 6 months, that's understandable. You don't have to be extremist about being green either. It's the total move towards sustainability and frugality that counts. We all have our small needs. I have a friend who lived an almost completely sustainable lifestyle down here in Andalusia and who wrote fascinating blogs about it. He lived off-grid and extremely frugally. He didn't even possess a toilet. Undoubtedly his footprint on this planet is very small but he did use green scratchy washing up sponges. Here you can buy Sparto grass bundles at a similar price, and they are much greener, but hey. If your pans stay black with Sparto and you like them to shine then that's your thing! And it is a little thing. If you can, grow loofahs for pan-scrubbers too. Its fun and green! These are the old fashioned but regaining popularity from green scratchy pot scrubbers. I've noticed that the scratchy surface left tiny fibres on my chopping board and I wonder what these could do to our digestive systems, especially if they build up. So although I used to love these, I've given them up. Another win for the natural alternatives. My 4 year old granddaughter absolutely loved peeling the crispy outer skin off a dried loofah and shaking out the hundreds of seeds inside. You can have that sort of simple natural fun for free … and it's priceless!

Many of us remember the two cleaning ladies on the TV using a combination of bicarbonate of soda and vinegar or lemon juice for just about everything. That's because they work!

Vinegar kills germs, and costs less than toxic commercial antibacterials, makes an effective anti-calcium deposit cleaner and a drain cleaner, and you can put a mix in a spray bottle as a general surface cleaner degreaser and chrome cleaner. Added to baking soda it blasts away stubborn burnt on stains.

Washing up liquid. I must admit I do buy the best-known brand. Largely because it actually is more concentrated and does go further. But I am open to suggestions on this one. I won't buy highly diluted liquids on principle they cost too much diesel ... to deliver water.

Floor mopping. You can choose Castille soap and a drop of essential oil for a nice fresh smell, or if your floor is greasy use washing up liquid .

Sunlight (the rays of the sun) is an excellent disinfectant so use it on your dishcloths if you live in a sunny place or have a nice sunny spell.

Active oxygen cleaner - chemical formula name Sodium Perchlorate. You can buy this as liquid kitchen cleaner and also as powder laundry additive. Buy large cheap unbranded packs. You can use this cleaner for disinfection all around your home, but it does have a slight bleaching action so don't use it on non-white fabrics and don't leave it on. Also, try not to inhale the fumes. I know I bang on about not inhaling stuff but this is important for your health. They never say that on the packs though so if you aren't sure, look up these products on Google!

Don't buy two types of laundry detergent. One for colours and one for whites. Just buy the one for all fabrics and add some of this active oxygen additive to your wash. I also use it for cleaning medical equipment.

Over-washing clothes is expensive but I don't like wearing clothes too long and usually only wear a T shirt, a pair of knickers or socks one day. There is an exception to this. I've found Merino wool doesn't only keep you fresher next to the skin but also as the second layer too! So an ordinary cotton T shirt with a Merino jumper over might last me 3 days instead of the normal one. It seems the wool over-layer more effectively wicks away moisture and prevents bacterial and fungal growth even on the first layer! The jumper itself can go weeks! And Merino wool socks can be worn several days too. See more on Merino wool in the Frugal Fashion section.

Home made abrasive cleaners

Add some a drops of washing up liquid or some Castille soap to a spoon of Epsom salt crystals. I have a little coffee measuring spoon in my Epsom salts tub. Use a brush, a loofah or some Sparto grass to scrub on if you need something abrasive. Rinse well of course. For a lighter abrasive you can use a touch of one of your white powders like neat bicarb or neat zinc oxide or kaolin clay. All of them are very mildly abrasive on stubborn and greasy marks.

Kaolin powder can be used as a dry shampoo to suck oils out of carpets or furniture. Apply, leave for 20 minutes and vacuum up.

Don't forget to save and cut up old T shirts and flannelette sheets, etc. for household cloths!

FRUGAL PETS.

Having any pet is expensive but if you have to have a cat for love or pest control (for us it was both) a sterilised cat will bring almost nothing but pleasure.

Here are some of my recommendations for frugal families with cats from our own experience. I'm afraid I have less experience with dogs. I never was a very good dog owner. I think you should only have dogs if you can commit to them as much as you'd commit to a child. Especially since they are also more expensive to keep and treat in sickness.

You must, of course make sure you can afford your cats inoculations. Expensive but worth it. Losing a kitten to a preventable disease is heartbreaking. Also every 3 months (approximately) they need worming and every month (approximately) they need flea treatment. Worming tablets are not expensive, but flea treatment is. You can get more for less online. I'm sorry vets but its true! Buying 6 or 12 pipettes will cost you much less than single doses from your vet. Watch out for expensive treatments that are just repellents. You can make those up yourself. I'm afraid the real thing is pretty toxic stuff.

Spaying your cats cheaper.

Female cats are more expensive to sterilise. If you are living on next to nothing you should still adopt only a sterilised cat or make sure you can afford sterilisation. Talk to your vet and see if he has a special rate for rescue cats. Or go and see your local cat rescue group and see if you can get access to any rate they have negotiated.

Antiparasitic ear oil vs vinegar and water for ear mites

When we first got our cats, we had to decide that we could afford spaying and their initial injections. At the time this was a rough call but of course we did it. We had to decide however at what stage in the future we might let nature take its course should they have an accident or illness that we simply couldn't afford to treat. We were going to find out very quickly that some medicines had alternatives too. When our new babies came to our home, we realised just how badly they had been cared for at 'home'. Home was a crazy cat lady who didn't believe in sterilising her cats and consequently had litter after litter to dispose of. Fortunately, she didn't believe in the standard bag of cats into water method common in Spain at the time either. Her house stunk and the cats, though loved, came to us in dire need of medical attention, particularly treating for fleas and ear mites.

We went home from the first vet visit with a small bottle of oil which was supposed to rid them of the ear mites which were producing a sticky black residue and irritating the poor kittens. Neither did they much like the treatment which consisted of wrapping their little legs or rather their 20 little claws in a towel. Laying them on their backs. Dropping oil into each ear and massaging gently to coat the entire inside of the ear. Much wriggling and head flapping ensued but, it seemed no ear mite death. A couple of weeks later we had to go back for another bottle of oil at another twelve euros. When that didn't work either, I'd had enough and consulted veterinary surgeon 'Doctor Google'. The advice I pinned my hopes on was the one which just seemed to make sense and that was the mix of apple vinegar and water. Within days our cats who had now had the full salad dressing were mite free! I wasn't too sorry about the several weeks of ear dropping and massaging in the end, though. Both of our cats are now extremely relaxed about having their ears inspected and played around with. Indeed, they seem to think that it's a treat. Both of them react pretty well to being swaddled and/or laid on their backs which is useful if they need any sort of treatment. Both are now very affectionate.

Asthma medicines and antibiotics

I have often been told that I'm being careless or inhumane to my cats using the following two treatments. Nothing could be further from the truth and both have been verified (off the record) with a vet. I told my vet very early on that I would be unable to afford long-term asthma treatment for my ginger cat. It turned out she had the condition and being a caring person and not just a money machine my vet gave me a piece of paper with a prescription on it for a human asthma medication, Theophylline. Vets don't want you to know this ... or rather pet medication manufacturers don't. To be quite honest I don't give two hoots for their bottom line when it comes to the health of my cat. Not forgetting the health of my and your purse. I believe poor people should be able to love and care for cats too, I'm letting this particular cat out of the bag! 1/8th of a 100mg tablet is all she needs and she only had it when she's really struggling: about once every couple of months. Before I get a heap of posts saying I'm playing fast and loose with my cats health remember it was a vet who taught me this trick.

Another time my other cat had an infected cheek, and I had no money at all, so I went to the internet again because I had penicillin (amoxicillin) in the house. This was from when I used to have bladder infections and needed it in case I had one while on a trip abroad. Our cat was in desperate need. I found out you could use a 1/8th of a human penicillin on a cat the size of mine and so that's what I did, for 12 days. In fact I've done it again since because this 'Floof' does decide to have arguments with rather more ferocious critters than she should and sometimes comes off worst. This time it was a long weekend and calling a vet out would have been extremely expensive. So I did the same again in spite of the infection looking pretty serious. After a couple of days the wound started to itch and my cat 'lanced' it herself which I thought I might have to do. Quite a lot of revolting blood and pus left the site, I bathed it and just continued the treatment. 12 days in total. I have in just one pack of amoxicillin - all the antibiotics these cats could ever need as long as they don't catch anything resistant. And I've just ordered my second pack of asthma medicine for my cat. She's now getting on for 7 years old.

Bathing vs not bathing cats

Your decision. One of our cats has long hair so we do bathe her about once a year. The other, we never bathe. You can use Castile soap instead of specialised cat shampoo. But be careful if you want to add fragrance. Very few essential oils are safe for your cat. You can use a little lavender or cedarwood which may also have a slight flea repellent effect, but avoid any oil with phenols. To be on the safe side do your own research or don't use at all.

You can also encourage your cats to use one particular garden area by emptying the kitten litter tray into one area of sandy soil that you replenish with new sand.

Keep your cats from veg growing parts of the garden using chicken mesh and pepper / cayenne pepper.

If you travel regularly make sure you have a cat sitter to visit every day. If you are feeling a little more well off we have found a food dispenser really useful and have always had one. We've had to replace it once in 7 years. Similarly, we have a water dispenser. Originally we had a fountain which was cheap but kept breaking down, so we found a big plastic globe water dispenser which is designed for small animals. Cheap and very effective.

Its always a good idea if you are travelling to have a piece of paper in your bag or pocket that says "cats (or dogs) at home", just in case you have an accident or illness

We feed only dispensed dry food to our cats because we travel a lot so the cats don't miss us so much when we're away. They supplement with lovely fresh mice, lizards and huge great locust type crickets. Effectively our dry feeding regime keeps them lean mean and wanting to keep the garden clean for us. We used to have both mice and even rats when the house was more unfinished. Now we don't! Also, I find dry food smells less, costs less and there is less of a problem with infections. If you have long haired cats you can give them a cat malt. Cheaper still is a little olive oil, or an oily little sardine every now and again … which my ginger cat absolutely loves. This is to ease traction of hair through the intestines.

If your cat has diarrhoea with a very smelly bottom, they may have problems with the anal glands. Before you freak out, check whether their stools are too loose. They may need more fibre. We've never had this problem with our cats because they have dry food and are not overweight. You can try dusting the cats bottom with white pure kaolin. Buy a little make up brush that you only use for pets, and dust their rear end with kaolin. It will absorb the odours, clump any 'matter' which is sticking to them and allow it to drop off and if they lick it, it won't do any harm, In fact it may help. The kaolin will be liable to clear up any diarrhoea they have. Kaolin, by the way is just very pure clay. If their smelly bottom gets worse you need to take them to the vet to have the anal glands cleared. Not a pleasant job but it can be dangerous to leave them too long.

GARDENING CHOICES

Get to know other gardeners in your neighbourhood. If you can't have a big garden, a neighbour may welcome you helping with their plot in exchange for some of the produce. If you have your own garden, you can swap your produce for other people's. It doesn't always work quite that way here in Andalusia where you give with no expectation of a return. But you do get a return because that's the way this community lives. Your return may be from just anyone, not necessarily the person you gave to. However bartering is possible both here and there if you develop the art of asking. Try offering money or bartering for good horse manure if you can find someone with a horse. I got 20 sacks of good horse muck last year for four English lessons. Result: excellent production in our garden this year! I'm planning to get just 10 sacks this year and pay money at the rate of 2 euros a sack.

Annual veg worth growing

Whatever the size of your garden and wherever you live you can grow something and the smaller your growing space the higher the value of the foods you should try to grow. Doing this puts you into a great swapping position with people with more space but easier to grow 'glut' plants. Here that would be *courgettes / zucchini, tomatoes, peppers and aubergines / eggplant* in that order. In the big gardens. We used to avoid these plants completely but now we do grow them just so we can grow and pick very early and be sure that no pesticides have been used. We get the baby veg from our own garden and when the neighbours come round with their big old veggies we thank them anyway and make them into soup or bakes.

Onions. We grow onions because they are easy to grow and they love poor soil (our soil isn't really poor enough now!)

Believe it or not garlic and all onions can survive cold winters from their roots buried under the soil. Plant garlic and onion cloves, sets or seed in the Autumn and they'll push up green shoots in the spring; leave a few behind each year, and they'll flower, seed themselves and divide their own bulbs to create the next year's crop. You will find its a better way to store a proportion of your onions than to bring them all indoors because your indoor crop can rot while your outside crop can give you edible alliums at some stage all year round. Sometimes greens sometimes bulbs. Personally I *love* garlic greens.

Herbs

If your garden is tiny or you have a balcony in England for example I would cut right down to herbs and maybe a few plants with attractiveness as well as food production going for them like chillis and peas or beans.

Basil - in a big tub. Harvest the tips first leaving the next leaves down between which the new shoots will grow. I taught my four year old granddaughter to count leaves before picking. I think I taught her to pick behind the 6th leaf. But it does depend how far your plants have got towards flowering. You need to pick them before they flower or at least just as the flowers start to show. The more you stop it flowering the more desperately it puts out new growth! You'll be surprised what a strong healthy plant a home grown basil can be and just how much lovely herby pesto one plant can produce! It is possible to buy a young basil pot and separate the stems into individual plants and grow them on to produce a mass of single plants.

Perennial garden herbs, fruit and veg

Chives. You can almost always get chives from a friend. They are almost as ubiquitous as the spider plant! They grow year after year but are quite easy to kill from drought on your patio. I know I've killed a few!

Bay leaf / laurel. Such a pretty potted 'tree' to adorn your patio or even your doorway. I once had a beautiful specimen by my front door, and a jealous neighbour poisoned it with bleach. Very sad as my recently deceased mother had given me it a few years before. You won't use many leaves yourself, but they are great for drying and packaging as sustainable gifts. In fact you can gift all your excess herbs.

Sage. Sage grows brilliantly in my garden and provides me with a mountain of giveaways but it will grow in pots and its a very useful medicinal herb and pesticide. Also look up sage butter which is an absolute favourite of my daughter-in-law making it worth growing for that alone.

Rosemary. Ooh what a useful herb. My husband boils potatoes in rosemary before tossing them in olive oil and baking them with other Mediterranean veg including slices of garlic. Rosemary is also blood pressure lowering which you don't want in excess, but in food quantities won't cause a problem.

Lavender. Grow for its beauty, Its medicinal value as a relaxant and for gifts and home scents.

Thyme. A lovely herb to serve with chicken soup (from the carcass).

Most fruit bushes and trees depending on how far north you live and how cold and wet your winters get.

Most of the foods we grow are annuals but successful food gardeners often also keep their favourite perennials. Year after year these favourites will provide reasonably reliable food crops with little maintenance required .

These are my own favourites which grow in Spain, obviously some of them including the citrus fruits and almonds are unlikely to grow in Britain except with special care in a heated greenhouse. There are some interesting methods of lightly heating greenhouses on frosty nights. See the plant pot heater in the home heating section.

Strawberries. Strawberries almost always give more fruit and more pleasure than you are expecting.

Raspberries. Rasps grow well in the UK. and have only just recently started to be grown in southern Spain but they're very successful at the moment in my garden producing fruit from around June right through until the very end of the year if you dead head old, spent branches. The neighbours who have given you their gluts the rest of the year will be delighted with even very small gifts of raspberries since they are so expensive. The only problem I have with them here, apart from they need lots of water, is that they can get sunburned! Make sure they aren't in a place where the sun is unrelenting for all the hours of the day.

Asparagus. Asparagus are a long-term investment plant. The first year or two you won't harvest asparagus at all, and each year you should stop cutting in order to leave a few shoots behind, letting them grow into the fern, flower and seed and of course die back at the end of the year to grow into the next year's harvest. Do not eat the poisonous berries. The ferns also make a pretty addition to a flower bunch.

Jerusalem artichokes (sun chokes). The tubers of this sunflower like plant have got a lovely nutty flavor and are delicious roasted, boiled, peeled or in soups. If you plant a single sunchoke and leave a few tubers in the ground each year, give the plant its own space and mercilessly root out any escapees you'll have a wonderful patch of sun chokes year after year after year. My favourite way of using is to boil in their skins. Leave to cool a little and then peel those skins off. I then cut in half lengthwise and fry them in butter salt and pepper.

I haven't found actual artichokes to be a productive plant in a small garden. They are pretty but ultimately a space-hog.

Chilli. We've only managed to keep them for 2 years so far but apparently they keep until frost kills them. This is fantastic news for my chilli loving husband and indeed for me as chilli has so many uses apart from adding spice to your food. They are medicine, insecticide, a pest and dog and cat training repellent, Xmas decoration and Xmas gifts and there is even one variety (the Biquinho which is an entry level chilli on the Scoville units at around 1,000 which isn't much, about a fifth of a Jalapeno) that I like to eat raw and I'm not a fan of hot chilli (although my husband is). They are very satisfying and ornamental to grow so why not, even if you only have a balcony garden. (Put your chilli inside in very cold weather). Contrarily a healthy plant will produce a milder chilli whereas an unhealthy one will produce a mean hot chilli.

Anarchist level gardeners will swap seeds and cuttings almost as an act of defiance against companies who are trying to stamp this out to maintain the 'purity' and more importantly the price of their own product. Hanging on to Heritage varieties can actually be important conservation work as well as very rewarding indeed. And if you're a local gardener in an area where pesticides are routinely used you may find that only unusual varieties are naturally resistant to pests. Where we live there is a typical ugly but delicious tomato which we just can't grow organically due to the many invading beetles. However an unusual tiny yellow pear shaped tomato grows really successfully here and of course its even more highly prized as a gift, being more unusual.

FRUGAL FERTILISERS

The main elements you need to think about in your soil are Nitrogen, Phosphorus and Potassium: NPK. Other helpful trace elements are Calcium, Magnesium and Sulphur: CMS. You don't need to have a degree in chemistry to get a reasonably heathy balance into your soil you just need to know what fertilisers add what elements. You also need to be vaguely aware of acidity and alkalinity and very much aware of humus and other decomposing organic matter which gives soil its structure and water holding properties.

When we moved to Spain our garden soil was dead. It was a building site, full of sand over a gritty and dry surface. The first thing we did was plant a few fruit bushes and then we added goat manure which a friend gave us to try to help them grow. That was 10 years ago. This year we looked at our soil and marvelled at how alive and wonderfully fertile it is!

Even if you start of with a dry sandy soil like we did here in Spain or a thick cloying clay like we did in East Yorkshire (England) you can end up with wonderful soil. After all most allotments are built on land that seemed at first to have no other feasible use. I'm not going to lecture on gardening. All this information is available online, but here are some of the ways you can improve your soil simply be swapping and bartering and using your own food waste and the soil's own ability to grow and regenerate its own nutrients.

Try swapping something with your neighbour for goat or horse manure. It really is gold for the garden. All manures bring weed seeds in of course, but if you leave the manure to mature in a big pile it will minimise the number of those seeds which sprout. On the other hand you can see the weeds as more green compost when dug into your soil. My last delivery of manure came with a large helping of ryegrass seeds from the horse's feed. I spread it thickly without knowing. When it sprouted and grew rapidly over a couple of rainy weeks, I simply dug the grass in. Later I found out that ryegrass is a popular green fertiliser. I had this extra soil improver delivered to me free. By the way you can plant courgettes or any squash directly into manure heaps or where a manure heap has been. They love it!

Ashes from wood fires and wood-burning stoves are a source of potassium. Other nutrients ashes contain in smaller quantities include phosphorus, a bit of aluminium, magnesium, and sodium, and a few micro-nutrients, such as boron, copper, molybdenum, sulphur, and zinc. So don't throw your fire ash into the corner or into a bin, use it! We burn wood from October through to April on and off. Depending on the weather a panful goes into the garden every other day or so in cold weather.

Dead stuff!

Change your perception of things that might at first seem a bit cringeworthy. We chuck our cats' dead mice behind our grape vines. Before you say "Oh yuk!" think about how many dead creatures go into making that soil *and* that at least we know the source of these. My Mum used to buy a fertiliser mix called blood, fish and bone. Pretty organic you might think but we don't know where those bones and that blood came from. Perhaps it could even have been from prion-infected animals for example. Death is an excellent fertiliser don't be afraid of it. Plant death and tiny animal death contributes to your soil's life!

Banana skins

I knew there must be something good about the humble banana skin when I went to a wedding in Thailand and the guest of honour (or entertainment) was a baby elephant. We were encouraged to feed her fruit and her favourite seemed to be bananas. Imagine our surprise when she peeled the banana and ate the skin. Just tossing away the actual banana!

Since then we've learned that banana skins contain a very high level of potassium and other phytonutrients. When simply rotted into water they make an excellent plant feed. Get a big black bin with a lid and throw your banana skins in to a puddle of water in the bottom. Leave it out in your back garden though as it does smell a bit although its not eye-wateringly rank.

Epsom salts

You know that the big tub of Epsom salts on your medicine chest list? It also makes good magnesium fertiliser if your plants are short of magnesium. You can also use it for a leaf spray.

Roses and other flowering plants love magnesium and adding a little to the soil around a rose bush helps increase growth and blooms. Sprinkle a tablespoon around a rose bush. This can be done up to once a month.

Compost additives

A mix of dry coconut fibre and bicarbonate of soda act really well as a composting additive. This helps turn your household waste into compost and the dryness of the coconut fibre stops it becoming soggy and stinky. The bicarb helps stop it becoming too acid and so is a good balance if you're adding coffee grounds.

Coffee grounds

Compost them for an added boost of nitrogen or throw directly on your plants. Be aware that rotting coffee grounds are a little acidic. Balance them with other more alkaline fertilisers (e.g. lime) or use more on your acid loving plants like roses, hydrangeas and blueberries.

Lime by the way is pretty cheap and so if you have an acidity problem its not an expensive fix. Most people just grow what grows well in their garden and don't worry too much about acidity or otherwise.

Also worms like coffee grounds but ants, snails and slugs don't. So if you sprinkle them round delicate plants to fertilise it also keeps the pests away. Double bam! I have read that mixing coffee grounds with their carrot seeds not only makes the planting process easier, but also deters pests. Presumably because the smell puts off carrot fly. And a little coffee in mushroom compost I hear feeds and encourages good mushroom growth. I haven't tried this either.

Egg shells and feathers

For a calcium boost to your fruits and fruiting plants for example, tomatoes, peppers and aubergines (eggplants) crush eggshells and sprinkle them into each hole before planting. Then, sprinkle additional shells around the base of your plants every few weeks.

The contents of old feather pillows. They work the same as eggshells. My mum swore by old pillows as slow release fertiliser for strawberry beds and other perennial fruit trees and plants. I use her method and have to say that the results are really impressive. I haven't tried any other method so I have no scientific proof but I've never had to fertilise my strawberry beds in any other way and only dig up my strawberry plants every few years to tidy up the beds, throw out any really tired plants and top up the feathers. I bury the feathers a full spades depth down in a trench. Fill back in and plant on top. Magic!

I have a rectangular strawberry bed. I suppose it's around 2 square metres and honestly its too big so next year I'm going to half its size which will still produce plenty of strawberries for two people to have fresh … and to freeze some. I'm told the eggshell or feather (calcium) feed prevents the flowers from rotting before the fruit is set. Often the flowers of fruit plants simply rot if there isn't enough feed or water for them to thrive. This is for the plant to conserve its energy until there are enough of the right conditions for better fruit. So, tuck up your strawberries and other soft fruits and fruit bearing veggies in feather beds.

Tea bags.

A bit fiddly but you can use the contents directly, especially on pot plants. Great for making balcony plants look attractive. This works best in warm dry weather. In cold damp weather they can go mouldy.

GARDEN AND HOME – FRUGAL PEST CONTROL

Slugs. Epsom salts act as a great slug deterrent as slugs don't like its sharpness. You're probably already using them as a fertiliser. Double benefit!

Toads. If you find an ugly toad hanging out in your garden, leave him be. He's your best friend. He eats slugs and other creepy crawlies.

Rats and mice. You might not like the idea of rats in your compost heap but if you find a pile of empty snail shells the chances are you have one. Of course the best way to keep mice and rats at bay is to have a cat or even two! If you want your cats to dispatch and not bring you their mice, keep them on dry food (with plenty of water in a dispenser), as they'll crave a nice moist mouse. Ours are vicious hunters and tend to leave nothing!

Baking soda as a fungicide. Add one tablespoon of baking soda one tablespoon of olive oil and half teaspoon of Castille soap to a gallon of water. Use as a fungicidal spray for your plants. A stronger mix will act as a pesticide.

Epsom salts egg shells and coffee grounds. All good fertilisers and all repellent to slugs and snails!

Sage. The smoke created by burning sage can be used as a mosquito and insect repellent. Used coffee grounds will also repel mosquitoes. Sprinkle a good layer of either in an old frying pan if you barbecue because the smoke keeps mozzies away. If you're just sitting outside you can use almost any essential oil in a vaporiser to repel mosquitos. These vaporisers are often found at charity shops; they seem a popular gift which people rarely use but this is a great use for them. I think they are also better than expensive home deodorisers. One of my favourite oils for all these uses is lemongrass and its not a very expensive oil. Just remember that essential oils are super concentrated and you literally only need one drop. Where they seem expensive they really aren't compared with scented home cleaners and deodorisers.

Ants don't like sticky things or powdery things. I've found you can even make inside out rolls of "gaffa" tape to stick behind units in a kitchen. The ants won't cross it to get on to your units. I've also had some success with simple blackboard chalk which they seem not to like crossing either. Nor do they like fire ash. Of course if its wholesale slaughter you're after then what my parents used when I was a child was a kettle of boiling water down the nest. Sounds pretty cruel doesn't it? I have done it myself with red ants. The other types that we have here in Spain don't bother me because they aren't generally very aggressive. And I rather like the extra large ones which seem to be quite playful. But nobody wants ants on their kitchen units or in their sugar!

Moths don't like cedar or cajeput essential oils. You can buy moth repellent wooden balls and discs but if you have cedar essential oil you can put a drop directly into the corners of drawers that you keep cotton and wool items in. An even better idea not to have too many clothes! In summer it's a good idea to vacuum pack your best jumpers. Don't vacuum too tightly as the creases will stay.

Aphids. To rid your roses or other plants of green or black fly, mix Castille soap and water with chilli pepper or garlic or any of the citrus oils. This can be quite effective sprayed liberally on the infestation. But don't spray it if there are plenty of ladybirds around. That's their job! If the infestation is particularly bad its worth looking for the ants nest because ants seem to 'farm' them. You can try a dab of vaseline on the stem of the plant to stop ants climbing up it. Get rid of the ants, and the blackfly will reduce. The sprays will also deter ants, slugs and snails

Chilli. A liberal sprinkling of hot chilli powder or black pepper will keep dogs from deciding to leave their mess outside your door or in your garden.

Wood ash. You can use wood ash as an insect or caterpillar dusting on the underside of leaves.

CHEAP MEDICINE

The word 'cheap' conjures up shoddy and useless. In a way that's exactly why I chose to use it here because we need to challenge that belief that in order to have any value something has to have 'value added'.

We allow ourselves to buy cheap imported goods because they often do the job. Sometimes that's only temporarily because of poor quality. We accept their cheapness, but we still know that cheap in the world of merchandise means shoddy. When it comes to a long-term goal like our health we are conditioned to think of cheap as valueless. In this way it's very easy for the medical industry to persuade us that we shouldn't trust medicine that isn't costly. That way we are maintained as 'consumers'. And health is a very profitable business!

The internet is full of magical cures for this and that. Don't be lured in. If something is expensive, it's not a guarantee it will work. Quite the reverse. Some of the best home health hacks are the cheapest.

The alternative medicines industry is just as bad as 'Big Pharma' for putting profits first. Don't imagine either that 'alternative' is better, no matter how much it costs. Neither should you be convinced that the price of a pharmaceutical medicine has anything to do with its efficacy. Sometimes there's a correlation with newness or cost of research. More than likely though, your medicine is just as prone to the price being connected to market forces as any other merchandise.

So your ill health can be expensive (and profitable). Maintaining good health need not be.

In fact, if the National Health Service as it exists in most European countries is dismantled won't it make us look harder at inexpensive alternatives? Here is a balance we must maintain. We must ensure access to the more expensive reactive services for acute and emergency services which the National Health is very good at. At the same time we must feel free to explore alternatives in the case of maintenance of good health and treatment of chronic illness, which allopathic medicine seems poor at resolving.

So there's my 'political manifesto'.

Here is my small contribution to your frugal good health. See also the medicine cupboard section of the shopping chapter.

You can take care of yourself and help prevent major problems or cure minor ones with all of the following.

Good food and water, adequate sleep and physical and mental exercise.

A huge number of the physical problems we in the developed world currently suffer from are down to two things. One is overconsumption of poor quality foods, and another is misinformation about which of these foods are poor quality. There is a belief that quality foods are expensive, but this isn't necessarily the case. Another misconception that people have about health is that more is better. If we are told that something is good for us we decide that only ultra refined versions of this individual nutrient will do. And health food supplement companies conspire in this misinformation. An example is turmeric. We are told that ordinary turmeric is too ordinary and not powerful enough to have an effect. It's true, it needs an added ingredient to work well. But that added ingredient is also cheaply available. It's black pepper!

We are told food 'medicine' isn't powerful enough. Well maybe it's not, on its own, powerful enough to cure an acute sickness but it certainly is powerful enough to prevent one. And it is powerful enough to ease a chronic one. Adding good food to any treatment is going to help (except of course when the best treatment is fasting). There are a few items you have to be careful about. Adding too many blood thinning elements to your diet at a time can be dangerous. Usually natural medicines in their food state, such as my example turmeric, will do no harm and will do good without serious side effects. Food is good stuff and we should be eating the best quality that we can get hold of. But that doesn't mean the most concentrated extracted versions of it.
"Let food be thy medicine and medicine thy food". Hippocrates

Please maintain your scepticism about whatever the latest fad or fashion in the food industry is. OK, but after all that good eating and exercise, which has many many health benefits, sometimes we still have minor ailments. Major ones, of course, are not covered here, and you should go straight to your doctor. Do not pass go!

The simple medicine chest

Some of the simplest items in your home medicine chest have more than one use.

I am very fond of some of the least expensive of the essential oils. Just because I don't have time to collect the plants themselves or distil their essences and because I don't need to have studied aromatherapy in depth to understand them.

Since sleep is one of the best health supports lets start with that.

Lavender: slows the heartbeat and relaxes muscles, reduces stress, promotes sounder and more relaxed sleep. It's pretty good against anxiety too.

Orange flower water is used in Spain to relax the central nervous system, creating a feeling of drowsiness and allowing you sleep more soundly.

Chamomile: calms anxiety and aids both sleep and digestion.

Chamomile flowers are one thing I have recently started to collect. They are easy to find and smell delightful and add an extra element to a winter walk in Spain or a spring one in the UK. They make a great goodnight tea, and I like to add fresh ginger root as my after dinner drink.

Coriander seed: rich in the B vitamins and magnesium, calming the nervous system. Fresh green ones from the garden are amazing too!

Frankincense: if your lack of sleep is due to anxiety put a drop on your pillow. I learned 'frankincense for fear' when I was suffering from anxiety

Remember that fresh air, relaxation and exercise are great for your health and may promote sleep, which is healing too.

Skin problems, cuts and burns: lavender is great for this too. For an extra antibacterial antifungal boost use in combination with tea tree oil.

Pain control: turmeric is an anti-inflammatory and can prevent or minimise joint pain from arthritic conditions. It *must* be taken in combination with black pepper and does not work well without it. It contains anti-fungal and anti-bacterial properties that may aid in the healing of inflamed tissues. I use it with black pepper and coconut oil as an edible medicinal 'drop' from the freezer.

A simple cup of tea can help over the counter pain medications such as paracetamol or ibuprofen work faster and more successfully. Best not to have caffeine in the evening, though.

I normally drink decaffeinated tea but pain killers only work on my migraines if I have a cup of tea with them. If you get migraines that are associated with allergies and sinus pain try taking an antihistamine along with paracetamol and tea. You can ask your doctor which may be best for you.

Sage in herbal medicine is used internally as a powerful antiseptic and anti-inflammatory. Burning sage in a room for an hour reduces the number of airborne bacteria by 94%. And that those bacteria stay away for days and even weeks. Citation: National Botanical Research Institute in India.

Aspirin was originally a natural product derived from the bark of willow trees but is now more likely to be synthesised Its a cheap blood thinner *but* it can have side effects. Check with your doctor before using regularly. I take a very low dose aspirin to keep my blood thin especially if I'm travelling long distances, as there is a history of heart disease in the family.

Ginger, fennel seed or mint: good for *nausea and poor digestion*.

Other self-help and frugal medicine advice

Dental work: contact a teaching dental hospital if you can't afford full price treatment. For short-term pain relief use a drop of clove oil on a cotton bud applied directly to the site of the pain but this is not a long-term solution. Don't wait too long to get a dental problem fixed as it will result in infection and tooth loss both of which are detrimental to health. Infections from bad teeth can be very dangerous to your long-term health. I'm sorry that dentistry isn't better covered on the National Health programme. It absolutely should be and would save the rest of the health service a fortune.

Urine testing

One expense that I think is worth paying for is 10 urine testing dipsticks. They are available online. You only need to test if you have any concerns maybe once a month or even once a quarter. They can tell you if you have any obvious infections or blood or protein in the urine, etc. Take the results if they are unusual to your doctor to diagnose. In my case I bought the sticks to see if I had urine infections. The strange results pushed me to seek an appointment to check for bladder cancer which I had. In my case they probably saved my life pushing me to seek help earlier. I don't think self-testing is very popular with doctors in countries where the health service is profit making. I wouldn't let that put you off. It may help you to know when your money is well spent. And in countries with a health service, it can save your doctor time.

Salts etc.

Magnesium (Epsom salts) taken as a very small quantity with bicarbonate of soda can help with severe indigestion. Look up the dosages online.

Sub-clinical magnesium deficiency can cause palpitations. If you have palpitations or little jumps you can try taking magnesium while waiting for appointments. You may even find that you no longer need them.

Vicks Vapo Rub is one of the few off the shelf items I really recommend. For colds and chest infections, it assists breathing and is warming. Its ingredients are both antibacterial and antifungal. I can't say if they are antiviral but I wouldn't be surprised! I well remember my mum rubbing it on both my front and back when I was young and had some bad bouts of bronchitis. My Spanish 'Mama' and my sister both say "put Vicks on your feet too!" Well, I think that's supposed to help with the colds and flu. I'm sceptical about that but having tried it myself I'm going to continue to do it. It's not unpleasant, and it also seems to keep my feet healthier. (Antifungal and moisturising).

This is a very short list of frugal health support. These are just some of the simple things I use, and there are many herbal health supports. Keep both your sceptical and your open-minded heads on when looking for 'cures', though. But next I've included some grandma's health advice.

If you have any health concerns that you are unsure about please go and see your doctor.

GRANDMA'S WISDOM – HEALTH

For your health's sake you should be aware of what your body wants or needs and I have to say the frugal living person should be less likely to encounter early onset disease. That said I didn't follow any of my own advice and I learned a few things along the way too. At present the UK, and where I live in Spain still have an NHS free at the point of need, but of course this may not always be the case and, some may argue deliberate, financial pressure on the service is causing big cracks to appear. My friends in the United States are not as lucky as we are and they face terrible privations among those least able to pay. Even more important then to understand that, bad luck apart, our health can be taken care of and that this is in our own hands. The more we take care of ourselves the less likely that we will get a serious disease that we have to take to a doctor. And for those of us that have to pay we want to keep our visits to the doctor to a minimum and to cheaper check ups rather than major chronic conditions.

Fortunately Granny has always had our back on this one. If not your grandma … someone else's has some good ideas which are folklore because quite simply they've been peer reviewed … over centuries!

Grandmas medicine origins and truths

"Feed a cold, starve a fever". Should perhaps be rewritten be feed a virus starve a bacterium. But Granny knew something here. In both cases you need to keep your fluids up but there is some evidence to suggest that viral infections are better fought off with adequate nutrition. You may even feel more hungry with a cold type virus. If you are really sick your body doesn't want food and this may be because glucose spikes can actually feed the inflammation causing bacteria and of course if you have ingested something infected there is no better way to rid yourself of it than to empty the digestive system completely which the body can be pretty good at doing! Generally your body will also know if you're ready to eat or not. Nobody needs to force an otherwise healthy weight person to eat through an illness but keeping hydrated can help flush out accumulated waste and is very important. If you have a fever you can rely on your doctor to make the call.

You've got to eat a speck of dust before you die. Not immediately before, but over your lifetime. Recent studies show that our over-clean guts don't process nutrients well and can leave us short of vital nutrients like vitamin B12 which can be hellish difficult to top-up from supplements.

Coughs and sneezes cause diseases. Makes sense this one doesn't it? But because of pressure from employers or our own work ethic we all race back to work before we're fully ready or even all the way through a mild virus but Granny would tell you that going back to work while your immune system is still compromised can lead to secondary infections, which may contribute to an increase in complications from these diseases.

When I was young we stayed off school when we had colds. Now pressure is on families for both parents to work and the kids to be at school or the childminders with what are considered minor diseases. The problem is that when the immune system is already struggling it's more likely that you will catch other infections and be unable to fight them off.

"Wrap up warm" and "take your scarf". Not so daft as cold nasal passages are more susceptible to infection. You don't necessarily have to keep the actual nose warm as keeping the rest of your body warm means that circulation will keep your extremities warmer. When frugal living you may find it difficult to keep your nose warm.

Hot water bottles and keeping warm in bed. "Sweating it out". The idea of keeping infections at bay by allowing a slight fever seems to be very common. Some African tribes keep new mothers in very hot rooms against post-partum infections.

Grandmas preventatives and remedies

Honey and lemon for sore throats.

Gargling salt water or clove tea for throat infections.

Whisky sipped or sniffed for first signs of a cold or flu. This comes from anecdotal evidence from the whisky producing industry where it's claimed that the people who smell and taste the product never get colds as the germs are killed immediately in the throat or nasal passages. These days you can get an expensive product called 'first defence' which acts in the same way as whisky fumes to kill early stage infections. I always carry a mini bottle of whisky with me on plane and ferry journeys and if I feel the tell tale tickle, or if I've been sitting near someone who's coughing a lot, I do the deep inhale through each nostril and a final gargle.

Zinc and castor oil on nappy rash

Lavender and chamomile for not sleeping.

Tea tree oil for disinfection

Hot poultices can draw impurities out of the skin and even cause a boil to come to the surface and break open. My mum would do this routinely if one of us got a minor infection, splinter or a boil. She had a tin of kaolin which is a type of clay. You could use zinc made into a paste with water or water and a couple of drops of tea tree oil, heated and wrapped in muslin or a lint cloth. Be careful not to scald the skin. You could also use oatmeal or oat bran as a poultice. The above poultice ingredients especially Kaolin and oatmeal are also good cooler, or cold for face packs. Mix with water for oily skin or with coconut oil and maybe a drop of lavender or rose essential oil for dry skins.

Kaolin has been used for used mild-to-moderate diarrhoea, severe diarrhoea (dysentery), and cholera. Kaolin is sometimes applied to wounds to help stop bleeding. It may also be applied to the skin to dry or soften the skin. As with all fine powders do not inhale.

Cheap drugs, for economic reasons, often aren't fully explored as gentle remedies and are in fact pooh poohed by the industry in favour of more expensive versions. Distilled concentrated and extracted drugs aren't always better than the whole food version which carries many other nutrients that work alongside the principal ingredient.

I have 2 very good reference books on my shelves. The Holistic Herbal, Daniel Hoffmann and Aromatherapy by Danielle Ryman. These may of course be out of print now but do beware of rapidly and carelessly put out ebooks, as I've recently seen some really dodgy and therefore potentially dangerous books on the subject.

My suggested home medicine cupboard in chapter 2 has a few ingredients you should always have to hand if you can.

CANCER

Cancer can be devastating even if you get through it and although you may not think it is a topic for a frugal book it certainly is. Quite apart from the fact that I wouldn't have been writing this book if I hadn't had cancer myself. I certainly wouldn't be if I hadn't recovered from it! It is both the prompt for the book and in itself one of my reasons to need to be frugal. Being frugal can help prevent cancer and other serious illnesses related to overconsumption, and can help you get by financially should the worst happen.

Although the complete causes of cancer are not and may never be known, and placing 'blame' for cancer on the person unfortunate enough to suffer from it is an emotive subject and one I don't feel qualified or want to have to argue, it seems perfectly reasonable to say that cancer can be the body's response to unacceptable levels of stress whether they be toxic, physical or emotional stresses or indeed more likely a complex combination of all. And I think, in my case, it was. The truth is that no-one yet knows what causes cancers and even scientists are still making their best guesses based on incomplete data. Data which sadly they don't currently collect. Nobody, for example, took any history from me apart from whether I smoked (I don't) or had ever smoked (I did). The fact that I worked extensively with plastics and colours was never collected and nor was my diet nor my lifestyle habits. I'm fairly sure my specific cancer (bladder cancer) is more likely in those that handle the products I handled in massive quantities. Additionally cancer may be more common in people who take a lot of flights, perhaps. Those who have a sedentary lifestyle or are overweight or eat too much junk food. Perhaps it's brought on by having had emotional trauma in a period leading up to the appearance of the cancer. People who are beyond a certain stage of life shall we say, for the sake of non-scientific argument beyond 50 on an incrementally increasing scale are more likely to get cancer. Although all these could be considered contributory, its unlikely that one single cause is to blame, although clearly one can tip the balance. More likely I imagine its more common in people who have a combination of these factors. I had all of them. Whatever the causes, its certainly true to say that more people are diagnosed with cancer now than were in my youth. The number of people expected to have some form of cancer in their lifetimes has doubled from one in four just a couple of decades ago, to one in two! This shocking leap can be down to the fact that we are less likely to die early from other causes and so more likely to get cancer at some time later. There may also be miscounting with people who have cancer twice, counted twice. Whatever the reasons we do need to look at what can lower our chances of getting and dying from the disease. But, and this may not reassure you much, those of us who don't die of cancer will die of something else. That's an inescapable fact. Maybe it's better to confront straight on that it may not be the worst way to go. But hey. Lets see how long we can stay!

My own cancer story and subsequent story of survival have given me a few ideas which I'll share. They are by no means to be seen as any kind of prescription. One thing I do know is ignoring symptoms or going down a purely alternative route of treatment would almost certainly have meant my death in very short order. I had surgery and chemotherapy both of which were brutal but I believe necessary, and I'm very grateful to so-called 'conventional medicine' for saving my life long enough for me to take back control. On the other hand there are also alternative ideas which I took in and which I believe may have helped.

Here are a few anti ill health, and even cancer avoidance and treatment hacks to consider.

Try to reduce stresses in these areas

Keep moving. Make sure you walk at least every day or swim or do other light exercise. This moves the blood and encourages drainage of the lymphatic system. If your job is sedentary it is even more important to get up and walk around at least once every hour, stretch and / or swing your arms too.

Don't wear tight bras or underwear because the elastic can put pressure on lymphatic drainage sites and slow it leading to a build up of toxic waste.

Don't allow inflammation to go untreated. This includes sore throats, stomach complaints, arthritic conditions, gingivitis (gum inflammation), sore ears.

Don't drink too much alcohol.

Don't smoke.

Don't allow fungal conditions to go untreated e.g. thrush, mouth thrush, fungal eczema and athletes foot.

Eat a good balanced diet with as fresh and natural ingredients as possible. Junk food is not cheaper by nutritional value than good ingredients, its only cheaper by quickly available calorific value.

Avoid ingestion, inhalation and absorption of toxic matter. If you are told that you should wear a mask … wear one. If you are advised to wear gloves … wear them … wash your hands after use and before eating … do that!

Don't use talc or any 'nano' sized powders. If you do use any wear a well fitted mask.

Do not inhale the fumes from burned fats, melted plastics and diesel engines (don't hang on the tail pipe of the car in front. That's dangerous anyway).

All of the above are pretty obvious regularly repeated advice.

I think we should add the following

If you have an emotional trauma or depression, try not to let it cause you to eat very badly and not look after the other parts of your physical well-being. I think that the way that emotional distress contributes to cancer is not direct but simply as a contributory factor to letting go of your own physical self control.

Check your own urine every 3 months using 10 test strips available on the internet. Anything worrying, take to your doc.

Take advantage of any free tests or screenings that are offered.

After 50 have a full blood screening at least every 5 years and ensure any unusual results are fully investigated.

Self examine routinely, but not anxiously, breasts, testicles, skin, etc. don't ignore changes.

Avoid sunburn, but don't avoid sunlight.

Alternative (adjunctive) medicine

Much medicine that is considered alternative was in fact, before the advent of modern drugs, pretty mainstream and a lot if it was known about quite simply because it works! Many people bunch together all alternative medicine as 'woo woo' and, while there are some pretty out there ideas which I don't agree with, tarring Grandma's wisdom with the same brush just buys you a whole load of expensive mainstream med-ications which can be less effective and more damaging. For example two very strong drugs with nasty side effects, one to counter nausea and another for nerve damage symptoms from chemotherapy, may be better replaced by cannabis. The jury is still out.

I'm not going to give advice on which of these medicines you should take … or leave but I am going to say that a positive attitude and an open mind can't do any harm. Myself I decided to lose a lot of weight and deliberately got my weight down from 95 Kilos to 70 where I've stayed plus or minus 2 kilos. The most important 'food' I went almost cold turkey on was sugar. I have added a little back to my diet now but to be honest I think I felt better without any! I also decided to try anti-angiogenic foods and planted loads of raspberries in my garden which I've been enjoying ever since whether or not they made any difference. I took up walking which I'd never done before and I try to make myself move every hour. And I started to be a lot more careful about my exposure to plastics although I still use them in my work. I can't say if or not those things had any bearing on my recovery but I can say that they helped my sense of well-being and my feeling that I was at least doing something. Of course I'll also admit that I was 'lucky'.

PERSONAL HYGIENE AND SKIN HEALTH.

In the shopping section (chapter 2) of this book, I have listed several ingredients I think you might find useful for your and your family's health.

There are obviously many more useful herbs and spices but these are the very basic ones that I recommend no home should be without. You can keep most of these in the kitchen and obviously also use them in your cooking, so that, when needed, they are easily to hand.

In addition to the normal kitchen ingredients, I recommend that you also have shea butter, beeswax, zinc oxide, kaolin and Castille soap if you want to make your own soaps and shower gels, etc. and a selection of aromatherapy oils. These are for medicine, cosmetics and just to fragrance your home and cleaning products if you want to. Since aromatherapy oils are expensive, I've given a list of those most recommended at the cheaper prices and those to bear in mind if you have a little extra money or if someone asks you what you'd like for Xmas or a birthday.

Creams

Zinc oxide is considered to be anti bacterial and anti fungal, however, although the non-nano version may not be as effective as nanoparticles, don't buy the nano version. Inhaling nanoparticles may not be safe (avoid inhaling any powders anyway) so we'll take the larger particle version just to be on the safe side. My mum used to have zinc and castor oil from the chemist for all sorts of uses including nappy rash and burns - freezing cold water is the best first aid for minor burns. Use to make a home-made cheap and effective all purpose cream for the skin. Mix with either warmed coconut oil or warmed shea butter and any soft oil of your choice (olive, almond, jojoba etc. but not linseed oil) and a few drops of lavender oil. This can be used for minor burns, nappy rash, severely chapped skin, or other minor skin irritations. Or you can use the same cream to treat itching, burning, irritation and discomfort caused by haemorrhoids or painful bowel movements. Non-nano zinc powder mixed with a carrier oil such as coconut oil makes a great sun block. Add a drop of lavender oil, and it's a baby's bottom cream. Add tea tree oil and you have a treatment for athlete's foot and other fungal complaints.

Keep these home made cosmetics in the fridge or make smaller quantities. I recently made some face pack for my family and didn't put it in the fridge and mine went mouldy! How embarrassing. It may have kept better with more tea tree oil but I think freshly made and used is best

Deodorant and anti itch for underarms and other sensitive areas like inner elbows, feet, upper thighs.

It will leave white marks, but these will wash off.

1 tablespoon of cup of bicarbonate of soda

1 tablespoon of corn flour

4 tablespoons of coconut oil

1 drop of tea tree oil plus 2-4 drops of ylang ylang and if you have it, rose absolut. If not, lavender is good.

Melt coconut oil and stir the rest of the ingredients together until smooth. Put in a shallow glass jar.

Apply like lotion and wash hands before dipping in to it again especially when using in areas prone to fungal infections.

Face pack

1 tablespoon of white kaolin.

1 teaspoon of glycerin

1 drop of tea tree oil

2 drops of ylang ylang

Rose absolut if you have it.

A little boiled water to make into a paste.

Don't add too much water. If you do add a little too much you can add more kaolin to thicken.

The scent is as above and these oils should also help stop itchy skin.

Pack in a shallow glass jar or bowl with a lid. Refrigerate if there is any left. Apply, leave to dry and rinse well to remove every trace. Or you can use it as a wash. Apply a little to a flannel. Rub on in gentle circular motions paying special attention to any oily or dry and flaky areas and rinse off with lots of water.

Baby sleepy time bath wash / shower gel (also good for adults)

You'll need 1 x 500 ml squirty-bottle with a cap. You can use an old shower gel bottle and scrub off the old label or buy an empty one from an import shop.

Liquid Castille soap

Fill the bottle. Add 2 drops of tea tree essential oil 6 drops of lavender essential oil and 4 drops of chamomile essential oil.

A drop or two of food safe colouring if liked. Stir ingredients together well and cap.

Bathing (and sleeping)

If you've had a tiring or stressful day add a couple of spoonfuls up to half a cup of Epsom salts and 8 drops of lavender essential oil and you have the perfect sleep promoter. Not only does it soothe aching muscles, you sleep better and you also get the benefit of a little magnesium entering through the skin and calming any minor heart palpitations. A magnesium foot soak can be very helpful at the end of a day on your feet. Some people swear ,and I think there's something in the idea, that looking after your feet is pretty good start for looking after your whole body. For kids the magic mix of magnesium and lavender in the bath can be a busy and stressed parents best friend. Use a coffee spoon of Epsom salt and just two drops of lavender oil in a baby or small kids bath.

Notes on aromatherapy oils

Make sure all essential oils are pure and of good quality. The more expensive the oil the more likely the cheaper versions are likely to be mixed down or even might not be what they appear to be. Lavender oil and tea tree are usually pure as they are common and easy to produce. Chamomile and ylang ylang are a little more difficult and expensive to produce so be wary of cheap versions. Rose absolut is very expensive so a cheap version will have additives which may irritate. Never buy any product which has all the range at the same price. They will not be pure, and you don't know what you're getting at all. Think about how much you use as one drop out of a few ml is not so much compared with the price of expensive cosmetics but you can't splash about the expensive oils. Nor do you need to.

Don't mess with aromatherapy. Only use these oils externally and always in water (baths) or in a suitable carrier oil. I have recommended only beginner oils and for just a few uses. Never use aromatherapy oils for pregnant women.

Aromatherapy oil: my most recommended

My top 3 which you shouldn't be without

Lavender - For nearly everything! The only one you can use neat. Disinfection, burns but most of all relaxation.

Tea tree - antiseptic post injury or pre surgery bathing

Frankincense - for fear ,for anxiety and panic also a very resinous smell can be used in place of pine

The rest of my top 7 some are more expensive and so a real luxury

Lemongrass - one of the loveliest perfume oils for the home

Cedarwood keeps pests out of your pantry and moths out of your clothes.

Vetiver to calm the nerves. A very woody smell. Use a drop on a cloth with a drop of lavender under the pillow for a soothing nights sleep. Or well diluted in a carrier oil (St John's wort oil is especially good for this) massaged on the base of the spine for sciatica or restless leg syndrome. This is a fairly powerful oil so take care with its use.

Rose (very expensive) another soothing oil. A drop on a cloth in your clothes or under your pillow makes you happy. You can live without this one at the price it is!

FRUGAL AND AVAILABLE. A FEW MENTAL HEALTH HACKS.

I absolutely hate saying this, but I'm afraid it's true and shameful. There really isn't enough mental health support in the UK now. And in countries or in circumstances where you have to pay, the cost can prohibit you getting the help you need. While waiting for the appointments you really need but can't get, here are a few hints that might help. I wish I could help more but I'm not qualified to put myself up as a therapist and in any case it would be a whole other book!

But try:

Reading **Matt Haig's Reasons To Stay Alive** for a personal account of Matt's own battles with mental ill health.

Pulling Your Own Strings by Wayne W Dyer. Out of print and very old but helped me through panic attacks. Incidentally, I don't recommend all his work but this one and Your Erroneous Zones are both worth reading.

Do not be ashamed of your mental health problems. They are no different from physical health problems. Lets not assess them as having any greater or lesser worth, nor any greater reason to be embarrassed or ashamed. I know that is easier to say than do because some people don't understand this. But that's their problem and not yours.

Quickie Anxiety and panic tips

I know 'quickie' isn't really good enough but I hope they may help a bit.

Please talk to your doctor and your friends and if appropriate your family about it. Anxiety was my mental health problem for a decade and these ideas helped me.

1) Trying to hold anxiety back doesn't work even though its natural to want to stop it, it's actually better to let it wash over you. Holding it back makes it grow like a wave. Letting it wash over you means its pretty quickly behind you and you can get on with the recovery.

2) Tell someone you trust when you feel a panic coming on. Even if you think it sounds silly. Try telling them that you feel like you're going to die of something if that's how you feel. You might be surprised how many people have the same experiences at some time in their lives. Even if the person you tell doesn't understand completely you really haven't lost anything because at least they now understand why sometimes you avoid situations. Sometimes you can even then laugh about it together. At least you've let the person know what it is you think you're going to die of, and you can tell yourself that they could maybe tell a doctor if you needed it ... You won't. But it's good to feel reassured. What usually happens is telling people helps make the fear vanish. It's like pulling the plug and letting it drain away.

Some very famous people have owned up to having panic attacks and you can go online and find out who ... and cite them in chats with friends. It helps to know you're in illustrious company.

3) Know that it is possible to get over them even though it takes some time. And the fear that you 'might never come back' is also normal ... but isn't true. Almost everyone who has severe panic attacks will one day be free of them. I can attest to that.

4) When you start to get some 'normality' back don't be put off by the bad days. Tell yourself '2 steps forward, one back'.

5) Right now forgive yourself for not being perfect. Perfect doesn't exist.

A few other ideas for general better physical health to help mental health improvement.

Look at your diet. Cut sugar spikes and caffeine both of which can make you more anxious.

Take the full spectrum of B vitamins. These vitamins support your nervous system and are used more by your body when your nervous system is under stress.

Alcohol and smoking can also deplete your B vitamin levels.

Eat a good balanced diet.

Do some exercise. I know sometimes it feels as if you can't, but really the exercise will use and remove some of the excess adrenalin and you'll feel better. Long walks, swimming are good. Park-run is great and full of people just like you!

Don't believe the "I would be happy if only I had more/bigger …" idea.

When it comes to happiness there really is no more than 10/10 and so being richer than you need to be, really will not make you happier. Adjusting your own opinions of what you need is a quicker way of achieving all you want than trying to make a million or have extensive cosmetic surgery.

Radical acceptance books and plans can help including 'The Work' of Byron Katie. You can see some of her chats with people on YouTube. Free worksheets are available, and they may help you with situations you find difficult to get over. The only work I don't recommend this on is fallout from abusive relationships. You don't have to take this all on wholesale just pick the bits that work for you.

I recently found this meme on the internet and its so perceptive I have to share it, under its author's name of course. (*@Nedwatarawwab*)

You cannot move on until you accept this.

You will not receive closure in every situation, but you can create it yourself.

Most of what other people do is about them, not you.

Some things cannot be explained.

Some people won't apologise because they can't.

You cannot change people no matter how much you think they need to be changed. People change themselves.

That's all pretty self-explanatory, but I think we all could use some of this acceptance philosophy.

One other thing I'd like to say about mental health problems is that we all have strange thoughts. Do not be frightened of your own inappropriate thoughts because when you get better they will go away quicker. You'll still think them but they will pass instantly as you grade them as both inappropriate and unimportant. The problem is when you start to think of them as awful and important they start to take on monstrous and frightening proportions and you think you must be mad, bad or dangerous. If you don't believe me, think about people who suffer from Tourette's which is a physical/mental inability not to express those inner thoughts. Tourette's sufferers are not bad people but they have thoughts which are inappropriate like we all do. We are lucky that we can switch them off before they pop out of our mouths. When you are under stress these thoughts might be more repetitive just as they are when a Tourette's sufferer gets anxious and repeats the same phrase over and over because it's the worst thing they can think of and they can't stop themselves. Let these people help you by your understanding that they are actually OK apart from that illness. And so are you.

FEEL BETTER 365 DAYS A YEAR

Something positive to do or think about. If you are depressed, discovering one of these on the plus side may remind you that things could be looking up!

If you're flagging tick one which might apply to you today. If you get one of these its a happy day! You can tick the same one again another day! If there isn't one that's appropriate for today why not try making one true. Or making a new one up?

Today I gave up a bad habit!

Today I gave up an expensive habit!

Today I saw a beautiful sunset

Today I woke up and smelled the coffee, (or just appreciated the smell of coffee)

Today I saw a beautiful sunrise

Today I saw a beautiful sunset

Today I appreciated stroking an animal

Today I told someone I've never told before that I love them

Today I realised that my parents really loved me

Today I realised what amazing people my kids are

Today I told myself that I am worth loving and meant it!

Today I told someone No, and survived!

Today I was kind to someone who hardly deserved it

Today I had a nice long bath just for me.

Today I went for a massage and hang the expense!

Today I gave someone who needed it, a hug

Today I started walking and realised I like it

Today I spent more than an hour in the garden and realised I enjoyed gardening

Today I got a bonus / sold a few books / sold something on etsy / ebay

Today I made a plan that I know I can stick to

Today I threw out some stuff I know I will never use again

Today I gave something to a friend and made them happy

Today I got a real bargain out shopping

Today I picked loads of veg from the garden

Today I treated myself to a pudding because I hadn't had one all week

Today is my birthday

Today I am happier than I was yesterday

Today I did a random act of kindness for someone I've never met before

Today I started a plan for a new income stream

Today I said sorry to someone and meant it

Today I found a bargain in a charity shop

Today I had coffee or a glass of wine with a friend

Today I wrote a story about something that made me happy in the past

Today I received a letter in pen on paper!

Today I sent a letter in the real snail mail post to say hello to a friend

Today I got a job done that I've been putting off

Today I tried out a new recipe and it worked!

Today I finished a book that I loved!

Today I got up late just because I could

Another way of making yourself feel better each day is to make your own positive mantra.

Mine at the moment is "Smart, Creative and Successful". It used to be "Healthy, happy, loving and kind". Or you could use Emile Coue's "Every day in every way I'm getting better and better".

Or "nothing good comes easy" if you are working through a tough task or a tough time.

HOW TO GET THE VERY CHEAPEST AIR FARES, TRAIN, BUS AND OTHER TRAVEL

For years I tried getting the cheapest fares but as the crisis bit, we found we couldn't book as far in advance. We simply didn't have the money. Also, the fares out were often cheaper than the fares back, and cash flow just made it impossible once luggage, insurance, etc. were added.

Then we realised booking the flight early but the luggage later was the answer. Yes, you may lose a few pounds/euros on the luggage, but only a few. You can effectively 'lock in' your flight price at the very best time. Buy your flight when tickets are cheapest and cash flow allows and then budget for the extras. And break down your bookings into separate legs and even into separate passengers to save on extras. I met one lady who booked herself and her husband on Ryanair separately so that she could check her husband in first. She then found out his random seat number and checked herself in with a seat choice, choosing to sit next to him. We always book our luggage late because we can't afford it early. This also means we only buy it when we really need it, and only on the one way journeys that we need it on. For example on trips home from England when we want to bring groceries that aren't available in Spain. Whereas on return journeys, if we wanted luggage one way, we were forced to buy it both ways. Unfortunately, the price of luggage from Ryanair has been steadily rising recently and now instead of paying 20 or 30 euros for a bag we have to pay 40 or even 50. However all my anxiety about late bookings have gone. I simply keep a careful eye on the prices and buy the seats when prices are good. What you save on the fares makes the extra luggage payment look very small indeed. Plus you never need to over book luggage 'just in case'. But do watch out for ever changing Ryanair luggage rules!

Also, it does seem booking as single journeys can and does work out cheaper. I can't be sure of this. It just seems to be the case. And it means you can book the outward when you can afford it and then save for the return. If the outward prices are very cheap indeed, you have very little to lose. To London from Seville recently I got two people for under 50 euros. That's around 40 pounds at the exchange rate on the day. Look at flying in to one airport and out from another. Sometimes its even worth using one company one way and another for the return. Always factor in if choosing airports which end it is cheapest for you to have the longest journey. You may find a flight to one airport seems cheaper, but the onward journey is expensive. Could you go further from home cheaper and take advantage of a better airport at your destination?

Incidentally check this when you book, but it seems to be cheapest to pay in euros from a country whose currency is euros. Especially when the exchange rate is favourable.

When looking for flights try all the searches. I recently saw the advice on TV that starting looking on Google flights then Skyscanner followed by Hopper was a good idea but I haven't checked this out. I do sign up to get email alerts of cheap flights. I live near Seville and recently got a Vueling advert in my email offering some silly (low) prices. Checking flights to Lanzarote from here, I could take a long weekend for under 80 euros return with hand luggage and an extra small bag. I can also get to the UK on Ryanair with additional priority for a similar cost. If the dates can be 'married up' it seems like a two hop holiday nesting Lanzarote inside a trip from Manchester (where some of my family live) to Seville could cost them around 160 Euros each return. Staying in Seville can be very cheap in low seasons too. Around 35-50 euros a night for two people in a small but adequate hostal in the Barrio Gotico, for example. This is just a sample but hopping in 2-3 hour flights from place to place is certainly a good way to get more experience for your money.

Taxis from airports. Don't always imagine that trains are cheaper than Taxis. This certainly isn't the case when two or more of you are travelling. Now with new taxi companies like Uber, airport runs can be very competitive; not to mention much easier and less stressful. For example we found out that in late 2017 Wakefield to East Midlands cost 70 pounds. Wakefield to Manchester 50 and Wakefield to Leeds Bradford just 35 pounds. Looking at the difference between the flight prices from the more popular Manchester to Seville route and the less popular East Midlands to Seville, we were saving 2 hundred pounds! Plus the cost of trains or the hassle of coaches made these choices obvious. We booked a taxi from Manchester airport hotel for two recently. It turned out as cheap as our other option of getting a taxi back the mile to the airport and then getting a train into Manchester. It's worth asking the taxi driver because if you get a nice one he can stop the clock when he gets to the price he quoted. This happened to us on that trip, and we saved about 4 pounds. He also gave us a 'talk' about some of the notable historic architecture of the city and that we certainly wouldn't have got on the train.

Skiplagging (America only) This is a trick where you save on airfare by booking a ticket for a flight which stops at the place you actually want to go but where the airfare is cheaper for the entire flight. It's not technically illegal but of course the airline companies don't like it. And you can't take checked luggage!

In Spain don't buy return tickets for the AVE *(Alta Velocidad - fast train)* as you can't get the Promo price on the return journey that way. We recently bought tickets from Seville to Madrid. By not booking 'ida y vuelta' we saved 20 euros each that's 40 euros total. A quite handy 25% discount, or looked at another way nearly 2 hours of working time which is coincidentally around the time the journey one way takes. Kick back and enjoy the film! Yes, you get a film and a free pair of headphones (In each direction if you want!). There are cheaper ways to get between Seville and Madrid and indeed all around Spain on the slower trains. You can travel as much as you like for 30 days, hopping on and off trains at any station, for just 88.90 euros or 60 days for 146.00 euros.

Train tickets: check out split journeys, longer journeys and return tickets.

In the UK trains are just ludicrously expensive, but can be a lot cheaper as return tickets. If you want to go one way to one station, and one way back from another station along the same line, buy a return to the furthest destination. This is a bit like skiplagging.

It's sometimes a lot cheaper or just pence more expensive to get open returns. Get together with friends and just give away your excess tickets. One friend of ours has saved us many tens of pounds with her unused returns. I guess we owe her something a bit special by now!

Don't dismiss the humble coach. For example a very quick 1hr 20 minute trip from Manchester city centre to Leeds city centre cost just £7 for two of us in December 2017. The National Express coach website can be confusing and it looks as if the price shown is for just one ticket. If you're unsure go a bit further through the booking process and stop short of putting any card details in until you're entirely happy. The Socibus, just like the National express coaches can be very cheap indeed!

Try Blablacar in Europe. Its hardly known in the UK. A car sharing site its like a paid for up to date version of hitching. Its much better than hitching for your personal safety because the drivers and passengers details are logged. You can have some 'hairy' experiences if you get a crazy driver, but if you read the feedback that's rare. Blablacar is useful for planning airport trips especially if you want to avoid car parking charges. Its pretty good for getting around Europe just for fun too. You can usually travel for half the cost of the train. You have to be pretty sociable and have a back up plan in case someone lets you down. If you have your own car you can make your petrol costs by offering rides.

ACCOMMODATION

You're frugal or you intend to be, so I have to assume you're prepared to compromise to get cheaper hotel rooms, here are some money saving ideas. My top tip is be flexible about your expectations. But do look at the reviews on all the platforms you're prepared to use. Remember one negative review among lots of positive reviews usually either means a generally grumpy customer or someone with an axe to grind.

Small changer ideas

Booking.com and Trip Advisor. Remember to search by cheapest first and my top tip is search as soon as you know you're going there but don't book on that day. Wait for them to offer you cheaper deals than those on the first page on the first day. Look for Genius deals which you can get if you are a regular booking.com user. All these kind of sites keep data on your habits. You sometimes need to let their algorithms know by your actions that you are neither desperate to use their services nor rattled by their last minute or 'just sold out' messages. Watch out for hotels that take money upfront off your cards when they say they won't. This happens far too often, and Booking.com don't seem to have a handle on it. Also watch out for accidentally booking the wrong days and for companies that cancel your whole booking without refund if you turn up a day late. It doesn't happen often, but it has happened to me. Even though they had managed to resell the room. You won't get chance to review that hotel for doing it because they mark it down as a cancelled booking. Stand your ground if this happens to you and always use a credit card or Paypal, which Booking.com has recently made available. If you do that, you at least have some recourse.

www.hopper.com

Hopper (add on application) is now also doing hotels. You can find the hotel you want on Booking.com or TripAdvisor and then check if you can get a little bit more off by going through Hopper.

This is more useful on expensive trips. Normally using Booking.com or TripAdvisor are more secure. Hotels can't afford to lose their good name with these companies. You often don't get breakfast all in though so going direct to the company can get you that breakfast amount which is where Booking.com makes their commission (by cutting breakfast to show a lower price).

Airbnb can be a lot cheaper but isn't always. Worth checking, though.

Frugalist ideas

Booking only one or two nights at your chosen destination and taking that time to find cheaper and/or better places.

Switching hotels at the weekend. Some hotels which are popular with city workers are less full at the weekends and some which are popular with tourists are more full at the weekend. You can save a lot of money by switching on a Friday and Sunday or Monday night. Most hotels, whether the one you are leaving or the one you are moving to will be very happy to store your luggage during the day of your switch. Also some hotels which advertise a higher rate when you book, will offer you a cheaper rate when you are already there if they are not full or have a cancellation.

Asking friends who live in the area you want to visit and offer them a trip to yours in return. Don't be afraid to ask. Asking and giving is not only frugal but also sociable.

Youth and other shared hostel accommodation. You will have to share bathrooms and kitchens and you may be in the same room as a snorer. Your possessions may not be as secure so you have to have the right mindset for this style of travel. If you are flexible and keep your valuables with you at all time even in the shower cubicle, this is a very cheap way of getting around. You also meet loads of interesting people.

Couch-surfing. Join the online group and in my opinion host someone yourself before asking to be hosted. It gets you over the fear hump. I've only hosted once so far . We hosted a young South American film maker and it was an overwhelmingly positive experience. Giving someone a great experience is really affirming and helps you with the idea of asking in your turn. Again you meet lots of interesting people but have to have lots of confidence.

Home swap for longer trips. Once you get into the mindset of Couch-surfing, house swapping is the next step … or vice versa. You can save a fortune on visiting some interesting places.

House sitting. Offer yourself as a house sitter and you can travel more for less. This can work if you're an artist or writer because you can tuck your laptop or your sketchbook under your arm and go. Usually, you have to like animals because often people want their pets sitting as much as their homes.

Frugal warrior ideas

Camping. You have to want to. I really do like camping but my husband doesn't. He isn't as 'up for it' as me on any of these very frugal accommodation tricks actually. He even draws the line at a shared bathroom. Tents are pretty cheap these days and are often available second hand, even for free if you are prepared to make repairs. Try freegle or freecycle.

www.ilovefreegle.org

www.freecycle.org

Tailoring your trip for the very cheapest accommodation, check out the Caminos in Spain. Whether you just want to get away from it all, or if you are actually a religious pilgrim. You don't have to be religious to do the Camino. Lots of people do them for cultural or health reasons. If you only stay at the donativos (donation hostels) you can get away with almost nothing for accommodation, but you have to ask yourself if that's very fair. It does very much depend whether you are actually skint or just selfish. If you can afford to pay something, in my opinion you should.

A slightly sneaky trick to get cheaper hotel or hostal accommodation in cities that are on the Camino is to get yourself a pilgrim passport. A lot of these places have extra cheap rooms for pilgrims. We got a very cheap room during Semana Santa (holy week) a couple of years ago in Cordoba. The city was extra full and therefore ultra expensive, but simply because we had the passport we found a pilgrim room. We were walking a couple of stages of the Camino, and the room was a bit grotty but it was cheap cheap! Its a bit cheeky if you aren't actually doing the Camino, but if you're respectful, and don't expect too much and aren't pushing out any other pilgrims ... More about Caminos coming up.

If you're cycling or hiking and using a tent try ***warmshowers.org*** Another group where like-minded people will open their homes for cyclists to get themselves cleaned up while on the road.

OTHER TRAVEL HACKS

Buy travel money before you go away. Its cheaper from your bank. See if you can find a friend or relative who is travelling in the other direction and wants to swap their money for yours. Swap at the median exchange rate saving you both 10-15 %!

If you can get a pre-pay card, there are some that promise low / no exchange costs and you should always pay in the currency of the place you're living.

Frugal travel cheap meals

Small changers: In chain coffee shops buy the one pound reusable cups and always use them! It saves you 25 pence a time. Have one extra large (venti in Starbucks) latte between 2 of you instead of 2 small coffees. Saves around 2.50!

Take a Spork everywhere with you and share cakes or even take them in and eat them in the corner. Don't be too shy about this but don't make it too obvious either. A Spork is a cross between a knife, fork and spoon. Very useful! Some outlets give them away, but they aren't very strong. One of my sons gave me my first Spork which I loved … and I lost and was very sad about it. Then my second son got me a really posh one as a birthday present. So I'm a happy Spork owner again.

Frugalists:

Travel kettle hacks. This is my favourite way of saving on restaurant and cafe meals. Make sure your kettle has no bare element. I have a nice little collapsible one. Note many European hotels don't provide kettles and strictly its against the rules to use them. I usually use mine in the bathroom in case the steam sets off the fire alarm. Take great care and use the hairdryer socket. In hostels you can cook in the kitchen, but many don't have cookers so you can still use *your* kettle.

Boiled eggs. Bring to the boil from cold. Leave for 5 minutes. Re-boil and leave again for a harder boil. Clean the kettle out well afterwards.

Boil in the bag meals. Bring to the boil with the bag in, then leave 5 minutes, boil again leave a further 5 minutes. If the meal is not hot, you may need to repeat. A pair of wooden tongs can be very useful, otherwise you have to tip the hot water down the sink to empty the bag out.

Don't forget you can make your own home vacuum sealed boil in the bag meals. I would NOT boil these in the kettle but just put them in the hot water each time. You really would need the tongs to do this.

Boil milk to make instant custard etc.

Heat coconut milk, pour into a bowl and add Thai green curry paste.

Frugal warriors:

If you have a vacuum sealer make your own sandwiches and carry fruit and salad veg in vacuum packs. They can last several days longer and you can content yourself that using the plastic isn't quite as bad as wasting food or as paying more for expensive meals.

WALKING HOLIDAYS

If you want a cheap holiday a very good way of seeing some spectacular countryside on the cheap is to walk the various pilgrimage routes across Europe. There are many 'tributaries' for example to the Camino de Santiago (St James way) if you want to know more about the St James pilgrimage there's a Hollywood film called "The Way" which, though somewhat romanticised, is worth a watch. You don't have to be religious to do a Camino. Neither do you have to be dedicated to doing the whole lot. You can do it piecemeal. I, for example, do a few days at a time whenever I have time or funds. There's something really rewarding about arriving at a new destination at the end of a hard day's walking and flopping down on a mattress. Any kind of mattress will do when you're that tired and it's a great exercise in appreciating what you've got!

There is a little expense involved in starting to do a walk like this if you've never done one before, but if you shop smart it really can be small. For example Spain has a sports shop chain called Decathlon which sells very good backpacks for between 20 and 50 euros. We have 2 each, a 30 litre and a 60 litre. The 60 litre won't go on Ryanair as hand luggage which is why we then bought the 30 litre. Even though it's smaller, it's a 'proper' backpack with the hip straps and the properly mounted shoulder straps. It takes real self-discipline to get enough into the 30 litre one so if you aren't hampered by hand luggage rules I'd advise 50 or 60. However, if you want to live a minimal lifestyle for a while 30 litres is just about doable but you have to pack extremely light.

Here's the good news, though. If you get yourself a Pilgrim Passport (available at various places along the routes, check on the internet) you can stay at many Municipal Albergues (like youth hostels) or Hostales (cheap hotels) for a lot less. If you're prepared to sleep in a dorm, you can stay for as little as 7 euros a night each. Some extremely basic accommodation can be even cheaper. If you really want a room to yourselves, you are going to have to pay more especially in the high season. We've found rooms in the low seasons for around 35 euros. Be aware you may only be offered a mattress, a pillow and a blanket so you need a sleeping bag liner at least. On our first trip we found one of these hostals and nipped out and bought a couple of small fluffy blankets each to sleep on, as the mattress was plastic coated. This may sound like hell to some people but weighing it up it means you can travel around for not much more than it costs to stay at home.

In the UK try The South West Coastal Path. Read The Salt Path and Steven Reynolds' books.

Before setting out on an adventure like this make sure you have the following:

A change of clothes and 2 changes of knickers and socks. Layer your clothes, so you only need to change the lighter underneath layers. A lot of albergues and youth hostels have washing facilities. If you have the clothes, you are wearing and an extra set of lighter weight, you can wear the second set while you are washing your primary walking outfit.

Get a pair of walking trousers with the zip off legs for several reasons. One part may need washing while the other doesn't. The less you have to wash or dry the easier its going to be to get it dry before you need it. If they match, you can take an extra pair of the shorts part without taking extra 'legs'.

Look after your feet and they will look after you!

My number one piece of advice is wear two pairs of socks and boots or walking shoes that fit comfortably over those socks. The reason for the two pairs of socks is not to keep your feet warm, but to make sure any friction is transferred between the two pairs and not to your skin. My other best piece of advice to pass on to newbie walkers that I picked up and its never failed me yet, is to take your socks off and dry or change them at every long stop. If you can afford it get a couple of pairs of Merino wool socks. They don't smell even after days of wearing. Put them on your Xmas list! I'm also a fan of Merino wool cardigans since a lovely friend of mine treated me to first one then another while I was ill and I now take them everywhere and rarely wear anything else. I quite fancy getting hold of a Merino wool T shirt.

You need a wash bag. Lightweight and able to hang up, including a very small deodorant. Take a tiny sponge a tiny squirty bottle of body wash (this will double as shampoo / washing up liquid / clothes washing) an extra small toothpaste tube. And a toothbrush of course.

A very small first-aid kit (just one between two of you) including a plaster, a small bandage, a safety pin and an ankle support. An antiseptic wipe and some Compeed plasters. You will need some scissors too so if you can find some tiny fold up scissors these are best. I've never had to use them, but they can make you friends on the road that is for sure!

A method of making noise, whistle or personal alarm. One each. I'd suggest if you're a man / woman couple the man takes a whistle and the woman takes a personal alarm. Try not to duplicate the same items.

A large soft travel wallet. One that can hold your passport as well as money and a credit card. I use one that's intended to attach to your belt. Pop it inside your clothes!

You need to consider how you are going to carry water. You need to take at least half a litre out with you. In Spain in summer you need to carry three times that. My son bought me something called a 'camelback' for my birthday. This a backpack water holder. You can get various sizes. Mine is 1.5 litres which is plenty for me on a hot day and enough for both of us on a normal day.

Sun cream. You can get a very small sun cream with a lip cream from Lidl or you can pay more in a travel shop. Don't pay more! You can decant some cream into a smaller container. Don't carry a load of low protection cream around. Carry a small amount of high protection waterproof cream. Every gram you carry is important.

I can tell you if you've never walked any distance before its an incredible challenge. Challenging because you get so tired and incredible because you are so free to stop and start when you want and to watch the world race around while you just take it in at a leisurely pace. You may even discover a liking for a cold beer at the end of the day like I did. I've never been a beer drinker before. I'm still not, normally. But after a long walk it tastes like a cross between total refreshment and nectar of the gods!

FRUGAL FAMILY TREATS

Treats are not only expensive meals out or big boxes of chocolates or buying another large plastic toy for your children.

For the kids

Rediscover playing together! Family fun got lost under the pressure of going to work to earn more money to buy more 'stuff'. If your family want to buy your kids lots of plastic presents it's their choice. But you don't have to add to that mountain of waste which you can't afford. Drop the feeling of guilt that the media try to foist on you and stick to your guns. Your kids will be the better for it. You can never compete with the richest kid in the school anyway so don't guilt yourself up trying and failing. Instead make a virtue of family play time. Plan for it. Share educational board and card games with other frugal friends. I currently teach English language using a lot of these kinds of games. The kids love them. Lessons are easy to plan and nobody knows they are learning and not just having fun.

I got my teaching style not from being a teacher but a play-leader. Here are my top favourite activities from that time.

If you get the chance to find an extra-large cardboard box (packaging from a large household appliance for example) give it to the kids, and some safety scissors, some felt pens, sellotape and maybe some old fabric. I guarantee that this toy is one that will give 2 days of messy enjoyment to your kids for no cost. It will probably be more popular as hour for hour enjoyment than a plastic princess castle

An old curtain or two will be great for covering your furniture and floors.

If you happen to have a stack of boxes, for example if you've just moved house or if you ask the supermarket for them, build a cardboard box maze. You can sew it together with string. Just don't go punching holes through cardboard with kids already inside! This is the best pop-up toy you will ever make for your kids and I guarantee that they will remember it for the rest of their lives. If you have a kids party coming up don't keep up with the Joneses by buying the most expensive adventure. Have them keep up with you by having the most fun! There is *nothing* in the world more fun than a surprise adventure. Sometimes to do this kind of thing, you have to drop your adult inhibitions if you have them. Most readers who've got this far have already got over that hump!

Kids love parachute games, but you don't need a parachute and the old king-size sheet will do. Just 2 parents and 2 kids are a big enough group but a couple more local kids will make the games even more fun (you can find parachute games on the internet). After all the excitement the sheets will probably be built into furniture forts, and you can relax with a cuppa.

Second hand: keep your eyes on the charity shops for construction toys, good quality family board games, roller skates and scooters. None of these things need buying new and yes adults can take a scoot down a promenade with their kids. Why not? Lose your inhibitions.

If you don't already go to the park or for a walk at least once a week that's another simple pleasure to rediscover. Maybe it became a chore because time was so short but if you aren't working now you have time. If you are working and its possible to shorten your hours by one or two a week you'll save money on the guilt treats you'll have to buy to make up for the fact you aren't there. Or use the hour you currently use for the gym which you also have to work an extra hour or two of overtime to pay for.

You'll be making way for old fashioned pleasures like pressing leaves or identifying bugs. Just talking about nature around you will open your children's minds and keep yours that way.

Learn a language together. Even, or rather especially, very little kids can learn a language and its not a chore. I have a method I use to get started. Get hold of or make an animal in a variety of colours, plastic cups in a variety of colours and play with the language around the animals, starting with what colours they are and moving on to where they are. The red rabbit is in the blue cup … In Spanish for example. El conejo rojo esta en el vaso azul. Heap praise on yourself and your kids when they get it right and be prepared to act the fool. It helps make it all much more fun. You can find basic language online.

Home make some sweets together

Truffles from the store cupboard

I accidentally made this mix while trying to make chocolate sauce for pancakes. The leftovers cooled and set into a lovely truffle.

A large knob of butter, one very heaped teaspoon of cocoa powder (un-sweetened), one heaped teaspoon of brown sugar. (instead of the cocoa and sugar, you can use drinking chocolate but its not quite as good). *One small carton UHT cream and one heaped teaspoon of custard powder.*

Melt the butter and stir in the sugar and then the chocolate powder.

Add most of the cream and heat. Mix the rest of the cream in with the custard powder and add to the mix stirring quickly to avoid lumps. When it thickens to a really thick consistency, take it off the heat and leave to cool thoroughly. When it's cool take a teaspoon and make small spoonfuls into balls. Roll in chocolate powder or icing sugar. For a more 'adult' version add a cap full of whisky or whatever liqueur you have in the cupboard … if you have.

If the kids are too small to help you cook safely, simply make peppermint fondant, no cooking involved. Peppermint fondant can be made with *icing sugar, a little condensed milk* (not too much or it will be runny!) *and a few drops of peppermint essence.* Roll it out on more icing sugar and get the kids to cut out shapes. They need leaving to harden the outside 'shell' for a couple of days but meanwhile the leftovers are always popular. Or if you want a quicker edible the cornflake or Rice Krispie 'buns' are a great treat. A bit messy if the younger kids stir too enthusiastically, but hey, I didn't promise happy frugality was tidy.

Incredible entertaining on a budget

Simple. Don't try too hard. Nights in with friends should be relaxed.

There is nothing people like more than choice. Just pile your table with locally sourced fresh vegetarian dishes (pates, soups, gazpacho etc.) and home made bread. Follow it with loads of tiny pots of home made caramel flan or the truffles above. Add a glass or two of wine or beer and your guests will be utterly happy! Any that aren't simply don't invite them again. Any that you think might not be, don't invite them in the first place.

FRUGAL WEDDINGS
(AND OTHER CELEBRATIONS)

You cant save on the following: registrar and licences. The rest is fair game.

The amount of money you spend on your wedding seems to be inversely proportionate to the likelihood of the marriage lasting, so be proud of your frugal wedding and make it an occasion to remember the love of yourselves and of your family and friends.

One friend of mine got married in a registry office, and he and his new wife went to the local 'caff' and celebrated over a shared muffin. Their marriage is so happy and loving. Funnily enough their frugal start wasn't a predictor of their future wealth either as they came up with some wonderful creative ideas together and published some books which they say have set them up for life. Although knowing them, I imagine it will be a frugal life as they are happiest with the simple things.

My husband and I didn't spend a lot more than that having married in the registry office. We returned to a local community hall, the hire of which was waived, and we spread the tables with some very cheap fabric, bought baskets and fresh flowers from the flower wholesalers and made our own floral displays with the help of family. Another family member made us a wonderful cake, and my (new) husband had made most of the vegetarian food. The food was very simple, just a simple buffet. I don't remember what we drank to be honest as our marriage has lasted so now its a long time ago. Our total cost back in the year 1999 was two hundred pounds.

A little more expensive was my son's recent wedding, most of the cost was a wonderful moorland venue with a hog roast, wedding breakfast and musicians. They still saved a lot of money cutting out a lot of the expenses with their DIY approach and, I have to say the doing it together bit makes the whole thing more, and not less, special. Some of their ideas are listed below with some of ours.

First decide on your venue. Depending on whether it's a religious or formal ceremony or not it can be anything from your own home to a castle if you are rich or if parents are paying! I'm just joking about the castle. You can and should choose a venue that means something to you because this day is yours. You want to remember it for all the right reasons, not for the stress of doing things the way your family expect and probably failing, nor for the bills both before and afterwards. A humanist wedding ceremony can be held anywhere you like for example. But you don't even need that. You can design your own ceremony and just comply with the registrars rules before or after if you want your wedding to be legally recognised.

Of course if you are getting married legally then you have to have a church or registry office date or book through a venue that is licensed to perform legal wedding ceremonies. The after wedding party can be anywhere that makes you happy! Here are a few ideas you may not have thought if before. A local community hall, a local park, the beach, you can just turn up guerrilla style and make any public space partly your own for an hour or two, although its probably best to check with any authorities that its OK to do so. But who can stop you and a few friends playing with frisbees in a local park even if some of you are dressed 'funny'!

Don't be afraid to ask your friends and family to help with the preparations. You'd be amazed how most of your real friends would like to do something for you. If you aren't sure about this idea, imagine if they asked you? How would you feel? Would you be delighted to say yes? Would you feel able to say no? It takes an effort in understanding to ask for help and an effort to accept it. And of course to accept no for an answer too. Those friends who you would feel happy in those situations with are the first people you can ask. And you may be surprised how many other people really want to get on board and are just waiting to be asked. Once you have that healthy mindset, you can achieve a wonderful party with the minimum of expense and the most feeling of pleasure and involvement for everyone. Someone might make your cake. My cousin made me the most amazing chocolate covered, cream filled, tiered wedding cake! It was all the more special being a gift made with love by a member of my family. Someone else might make a dress. Someone else might arrange the flowers. You might have friends in a band. If you would do it for your friends, gratefully accept them doing it for you. As for twittery parents. They're always better occupied being given a job to do!

My daughter in law saved a lot of money by having parties with friends where they made hand crafted wedding items. You can make your own.

Cake and cake topper, packs of biodegradable confetti (rose petals, rice etc.), wedding breakfast decorations, place mats and invitations, flowers and bridal favours. You can also ask friends to help out with bringing multi-use items for example they could bring white or coloured sheets or curtain fabric which can first be used for table covers and then for your future home, instead of conventional wedding presents. If you're a frugalist with a passion for making jam, pickles or preserves you could ask for Mason / Kilner jars and fill them with flowers or candles.

Photography - ask all friends to share any pictures they take or nominate a creative friend as your photographer. Find a photography course for them on a group like Skillshare. Maybe gift a creative friend a subscription to such a course if she / he would enjoy that.

In the unlikely event that you find you and your partner simply can't agree on anything, or compromise on anything or do anything together for the wedding, that too may give you an indication of whether or not you're making the right decision.

I truly believe the more you get involved in the preparation and presentation of your own wedding, the more likely the time you spend together with your partner and best friends will set you up for a more successful marriage and social life.

FRUGAL XMAS

A lot of our parents and grandparents used to start buying for Xmas right back at the beginning of the year. This is an idea with a very long history from when long winters meant very harsh conditions and little food or comfort. Some might say the origins of Xmas are the time in the middle of winter when you opened up your stores and allowed yourself to start using the saved items. Well, it's now quite fashionable to have quirky old-fashioned decorations and presents, so you can create a magical Xmas frugally.

You can also consider a crafty Xmas present swap. This is where you decide to make a number of Xmas present or decoration items and swap them with friends who make other things that you think your friends or relatives might like.

I am often driven by things that seemed magical in my own childhood, because its almost always the less expensive creations that filled my little head with wonder and made my eyes sparkle. One of my very special Xmas memories is when a teacher brought in twigs and white paint and we spent the whole session painting twigs white. We then hung them with home made wool bobbles that we'd made in a previous class. Magical!

Start a present and card drawer. Throw in things you've seen that you know someone you love will like. Make cards. Throw them in there too. Throw notes about what people have enjoyed before or something you've just found out. Put in old wrapping paper, ribbons and decorative items.

Second-hand items for your frugal friends. Worth looking out for in charity shops:

Slow cooker, rice cooker, bread maker, vacuum sealer. Check they haven't already got these items!

To me every Xmas has to have a tree of some kind. The smell of pine and the process of decorating. I finally relented and got a good quality fake tree. This was about 15 years ago, so it's cost me about 3 pounds a year so far. This tree had real pine cones wired to it. Every year I put a drop of pine essential oil on half the cones and a drop of orange essential oil on the other half. If you can find a pine forest (luckily I have one a couple of hundred yards away) you can collect your own pine cones and wire them to your tree or hang them from painted twigs. You can get hemp or jute cord cheaply online and it has loads of Xmas uses.

Wrapping presents in newsprint or brown paper and adding jute / hemp ties and pine cones is a cool way to go both frugal and green. Even the wealthy are adopting some of these frugal designs because they reek of comfort and midwinter charm. Frugality and green and sustainable are very fashionable for Xmas if at no other time of the year!

If you have a group of frugal or crafting friends, you can get together and swap ideas or craft together for Xmas.

How about calling a 'sustainable Xmas' this year and if it works, make it a regular thing. This year I'm making home made presents for everyone including the grandchildren. They are getting a bath time kit. One very long but unpeeled (dried) loofah between them and instructions to the parents to chop it in half so that the 3 year old, and the 4 year old can peel their half and empty the seeds out and rinse it ready for use. I know they enjoy this because they peeled and emptied one the last time they were here. Then I'm making them their own liquid soap with Castile soap with a few drops of lavender and tea tree essential oils. If I get time, I'll decorate the bottles too.

The parents are getting a stocking full of little presents. More loofah pieces for the washing up. Wax wraps for the kitchen. Home-grown chillis of all varieties and maybe some home made Xmas tree decorations this year made from wound string. I started giving my family Xmas decorations a few years ago when I was unsure of my health. I wanted to give them my favourite ones in case I wasn't there the following year. Well, I was still here, so they now get more decorations each year. I've also decided on my frugal Xmas there should be some obviously frugal but attractive decorations too. Some of my friends are getting a little packet of loofah seeds in with their Xmas cards. I also made some lovely scented fresh cosmetics.

Oh and don't forget to buy them a copy of this book for Xmas! (Well you gotta try!)

LUXURIES TO PUT ON YOUR XMAS OR BIRTHDAY LIST.

If non-frugal members of your family want to help you with your frugal goals here are some gifts the more generous ones could give you. If they don't understand them, just suggest the essential oils are a luxury you can't afford. They are a real pleasure to receive and can be made into both luxury and ordinary household and medicinal items.

Smaller price items

Aromatherapy oils (pure essential)

Cheaper ones include: lavender, lemon, lemongrass, pine, orange, neroli, mint.

Medium price: cedar, vetivert, frankincense

High price: rose absolut

Carrier oils and other oils etc. for cosmetic making:

Almond oil

Coconut oil

Jojoba oil

Shea butter

Beeswax

There is more about how to use all these in the health and personal care and household sections of this book.

Very high priced items for generous relatives to get you or for you to buy yourself if you get an unexpected windfall. These will make your life easier.

(Tell your friends / relatives you are happy with second hand!)

A kitchen system like Cecotec Mambo (my recommended cheaper version of the Thermomix) absolutely fantastic for frugal meal making especially soups for garden and cheap in-season veggies approx 170 euros.

A slow cooker.

Vacuum sealing machine and bags. Approx 60 euros (cheaper in Lidl when available).

Robot vacuum cleaner. Yes honestly! They are very efficient. Save electricity, especially if you're off-grid or on an economy tariff, save time and are great if you have pets and or asthma. I recommend Cecotec

Conga approx 150 euros. No use if you have really deep carpets or really tiny rooms. Excellent if you have tiled floors and especially in summer. More about this back in Grandmas Wisdom - Health.

Kindle or tablet with Kindle installed if you don't already have one. Especially good if it also has your social media and email on it. There is no luxury greater than reading in bed!

POSTSCRIPT

Having read through the book more often than I really cared to, I do think that there may be some perception of an implied criticism of anyone who is forced to or who chooses to work the standard 35-40 hour working week. Actually I am really pleased that in my lifetime that seems to have come down from 40 to nearer 35. I want to be clear that the choice of how many hours a day to work is entirely a personal decision and I'm a bit of a workaholic myself and have missed many opportunities to spend more time with the kids. My argument is not with how long people choose to work, but more with the inflexible system that means there is little choice and the similarly inflexible belief that leads some people to think that those who work under less pressure for around for 12 hours a day instead of working in a specific building under strip lights on a fixed contract are somehow not "knuckling down". Or that those among us who have different values are trying to destroy their values.

It *is* time to look with more flexible attitudes to the work life balance and with more understanding of the value of milking life for every drop of human happiness that it contains. In the end we should value choice and difference. We should value abilities in all different areas. The ability of the simple Grandma in her simple home with the children and the meat pie and the clock seemingly ticking more slowly than everyone else's has a value no greater nor lesser than the woman in a smart business suit and high heels, has the same value as the slightly bonkers inventor, has the same value as the politician in her halls. No more and no less.

My criticism is that our inability to realise that making pejorative judgements on lifestyle choices does nothing to increase our own happiness or that of our fellow man. Money is a false value in the pursuit of human happiness. Nevertheless it's the playground we are all playing in and one of the the currencies we all have to play with. How you play with it or use it for change is the choice you have to make and you have to be more creative with those choices the less that you have but it is not the only item of value we have to play with.

I like an expression my son shared with me one day when we were talking about the way someone was behaving and he said "That's their currency" meaning, I believe, the thing or the behaviour that has a power value, that they are moulding their world with. I found this an interesting concept and it's an expression I will always remember. Think about the value of stopping for a moment, taking a breath, listening to your kids and to your parents and grandparents. Listen to your friends and those you don't always agree with. When they give you their time to listen to you or explain things to you they are giving you their currency. The value of that gift is both infinitely small and infinitely great at the same time It is in a sense, Shroedinger's currency.

THANKS AND ACKNOWLEDGEMENTS

I want to thank everyone who has encouraged me to write this book which is outside my usual sphere … and the next one which is coming up quickly on its heels. I especially want to thank the grumpy old men and women in my family and those who I meet through my work and on Facebook etc. People who tell it like it is, but with a good dollop of empathy, inspire me. And to Eddie Willson whose 2006 'zine 'Poor But Happy' triggered the idea in me of valuing all of my hours. I'd like to thank Pat Goodall-McIntosh, recently deceased but who until almost her last breath was encouraging and made a special effort to tell me to continue writing even though, as she said herself, some of my writing errors and deliberate rule breaking (usually errors) drove her crazy.

I also want to thank members of my own family who have shown interest in my creativity and actively and emotionally supported it through some recent tough years. Those who have listened and given me snippets of their wisdom and insights. My daughter, who tells me off for writing errors regularly and I find I now enjoy it! My son mentioned in the postscript. And the rest of my hard working family whose difficult and wise choices have inspired me too. My friend with whom I have long and sometimes uneasy conversations, and who forces me to look at the other side of every argument. I'd like to thank my cousin who just makes me feel loved and valued.

I want to thank my Patrons. Some are already mentioned above and many have now been with me for nearly 2 years. Your support has made this and other creative work possible. Among them:

Riemkje Boom-Oosterhof, Susan Wegbreit Martinsen, Ann Storey, Maryse Cuypers, Natalie Martin-Burrows, Denise Osborne, Stephanie Ryan, Rosemary Mulley, Gillian Mason Thompson, Anke Humpert, Karen Tiberius Rollinson, Netta Murphy, Lesley Symonds, Roberta Solari, Toni Ballinger, Helen Cruickshank, Tukta Nodame

And others who prefer not to be mentioned. Thank you all!

And of course I want to thank my long suffering husband without who all my creative efforts would just be piles of unrelenting drivel with no outlet or purpose. I'm not being falsely modest here. He really does have to pull my output into shape, otherwise he'd drown under half finished projects and daft ideas.

Get my latest rants at
www.facebook.com/Littleoldladywho

or follow on Twitter
twitter.com/Littleoldladyw1